THE CONDITION OF CITIZENSHIP

Politics and Culture

A Theory, Culture & Society series

Politics and Culture analyses the complex relationships between political institutions, civil society and contemporary states. Individual books will draw on the major theoretical paradigms in sociology, politics and philosophy within which citizenship, rights and justice can be understood. The series will focus attention on the importance of culture and the implications of globalization and postmodernism for the study of politics and society. It will relate these advanced theoretical issues to conventional approaches of welfare, participation and democracy.

SERIES EDITOR: Bryan S. Turner, *Deakin University*

EDITORIAL BOARD
J.M. Barbalet, *Australian National University*
Mike Featherstone, *University of Teesside*
Stephen Kalberg, *Boston University*
Carole Pateman, *University of California, Los Angeles*

Also in this series

Welfare and Citizenship
Beyond the Crisis of the Welfare State?
Ian Culpitt

Citizenship and Social Theory
edited by Bryan S. Turner

THE CONDITION OF CITIZENSHIP

edited by

Bart van Steenbergen

SAGE Publications
London • Thousand Oaks • New Delhi

First published 1994

SAGE Publications Ltd
6 Bonhill Street
London EC2A 4PU

SAGE Publications Inc
2455 Teller Road
Thousand Oaks, California 91320

SAGE Publications India Pvt Ltd
32, M-Block Market
Greater Kailash – I
New Delhi 110 048

British Library Cataloguing in Publication data

Condition of Citizenship. – (Politics &
Culture Series)
 I. Steenbergen, Bart Van II. Series
 323.6

ISBN 0–8039–8881–8
ISBN 0–8039–8882–6 (pbk)

Library of Congress catalog card number 93–087423

Typeset by Photoprint, Torquay, Devon
Printed in Great Britain by Biddles Ltd, Guildford, Surrey

CONTENTS

CONTRIBUTORS

Hans Adriaansens is Professor of General Social Sciences at the University of Utrecht and member of The Netherlands Scientific Council for Government Policy. He is the author of *General Sociology* (1985) and *Participation State* (1990).

Attila Agh is Professor of Political Science at the Budapest University of Economics. He is author of *The Crisis of State Socialism in the Eighties* (1990).

Ralf Dahrendorf is Warden of Saint Antony's College in Oxford. He is author of *The Modern Social Conflict* (1988) and *Reflections on the Revolution in Europe* (1990).

Richard Falk is Professor of International Relations at Princeton University and Research Director of the World Order Models Project. He is author of *A Study of Future Worlds* (1975) and *Explorations at the Edge of Time: Prospects for World Order* (1992).

Nancy Fraser is Professor of Philosophy and Faculty Fellow of the Center for Urban Affairs and Policy Research at Northwestern University. She is author of *Unruly Practices* (1989) and the co-editor of *Revaluing French Feminism* (1988).

Linda Gordon is Professor of History at the University of Wisconsin. Among her books are *Woman's Body, Woman's Right: a Social History of Birth Control; Heroes of their own Lives: the Politics of Family Violence*; and *Pitied but not Entitled: Single Mothers and the History of Welfare* (1994).

Herman van Gunsteren is Professor of Theory and Jurisprudence at the University of Leiden. He is the author of 'The quest for control' in *Ethics*, July 1988 and co-author of *Time for Retirement* (1991).

Jürgen Habermas is Professor of Philosophy at the University of Frankfurt. He is author of *The Theory of Communicative Action* (1989) and *The Structural Transformation of the Public Sphere* (1989).

Bart van Steenbergen is Associate Professor of General Social Sciences at the University of Utrecht. He is co-author of *Advancing Democracy and Participation: Challenges for the Future* (1992) and 'Scenarios for Europe in the 1990s: the role of citizenship and participation' in *Futures*, November 1990.

Bryan S. Turner is Professor of Sociology at Deakin University. He is author of *Citizenship and Capitalism* (1986) and 'Outline of a theory of citizenship' in *Sociology*, May 1990.

Ursula Vogel is Senior Lecturer in Government at the University of Manchester. She is co-editor of *Feminism and Political Theory* (1986) and of *The Frontiers of Citizenship* (1991) and author of 'Patriarchal reasoning in modern natural law' in *History of Political Thought* (1991).

William Julius Wilson is the Lucy Flower University Professor of Sociology and Public Policy at the University of Chicago. He is author of *The Truly Disadvantaged* (1987) and *The Declining Significance of Race* (1978).

1

THE CONDITION OF CITIZENSHIP: AN INTRODUCTION

Bart van Steenbergen

Most recent publications on citizenship begin by expressing surprise that this subject has suddenly become topical. Over the past five years, more and more social problems and questions have been formulated in terms of citizenship and civil society. Whether the subject is poverty, the underclass, women's issues, national identity, participatory democracy, minorities, authoritarian governments, supranational developments, the role of the intelligentsia and even the environment, it seems that all these problems can be fruitfully analysed from the perspective of citizenship. On the other hand, there also seems to be agreement that citizenship is a problematic concept. Its meaning has never been univocal; on the contrary, there are several historical traditions in this respect, which in some ways oppose each other, as the contributions of van Gunsteren (Chapter 4) and Habermas (Chapter 3) elucidate.

This book is not so much about citizenship as such, nor about the history of citizenship, although some contributors deal with these topics, but primarily about the question of the fruitfulness of the notion of citizenship for analysing, understanding and even solving the problems of our time and of the time to come. As we shall see, the traditional concepts are not always fully fit for that purpose, although we can find much in the old concepts that is still valuable for our time.

Although this book is not about citizenship as such, a few words on the concept itself may be illuminating, not least because different authors in this book base themselves on different traditions in this respect. To start with, a distinction (but not a separation) should be made between the citizen or *citoyen*, on the one hand, and the burgher, bourgeois or economic citizen on the other as the chief actors or 'dramatis personae' to use Agh's terminology (see Chapter

9), of social, political and economic life in modern Western societies.

Citizenship represents the notion of participation in public life (which is broader than political life). In particular, since Marshall's definition of the ideal of citizenship as full participation in the community, we can see a definite shift from a strict political definition of a citizen – with an emphasis on his or her relationship with the state – to a broader somewhat more sociological definition, which implies a greater emphasis on the relationship of the citizen with society as a whole.

Secondly, a citizen is a person who both governs and is governed, for which qualifications like autonomy, judgement and loyalty are expected. In that sense citizenship is an 'office' for which one has to qualify as van Gunsteren (Chapter 4) emphasizes.

Thirdly, and related to the former two, is that citizenship deals with rights and entitlements on the one hand and with obligations on the other. Some authors, and in particular Dahrendorf (Chapter 2), stress the entitlements of citizens *vis à vis* the state, which can be seen as the 'entrance component', whereas others emphasize the other side of the coin, the responsibility of the citizen for the community. Ideally, a citizen is active in public life and fundamentally willing to submit his private interests to the general interest of society, whereas a burgher or economic citizen generally lacks this feeling of responsibility and public spirit. In these distinctions we can recognize the different philosophical traditions of citizenship: the liberal-individualistic, the republican and the communitarian one (see especially van Gunsteren in Chapter 4).

One of the classic texts on citizenship, to which many of the authors in this book regularly refer, is T.H. Marshall's essay on 'Citizenship and social class' (1949). Marshall distinguishes here three types of citizenship, which emerged during the past three centuries in such a way that each new type was standing on the shoulder of its predecessor.

In the eighteenth century the first type emerged: *civil citizenship*, which established the rights necessary for individual freedom, such as rights to property, personal liberty and justice. The second type, *political citizenship*, was built primarily in the nineteenth century and encompassed the right to participate in the exercise of political power. The third type, *social citizenship*, was constructed in the twentieth century. This type emphasized the citizen's rights of economic and social security and gained its expression in the modern welfare state as it developed in Western Europe.

For our purpose it is important to note that, according to Marshall, this last type marked the *final* stage of this development.

With the coming of social citizenship, the ultimate ideal of citizenship, the full participation of the individual in the community could be realized. It should be stressed that there is a fundamental difference between the principles of a liberal and democratic society, based on civil and political rights on the one hand and the social rights as expressed in the welfare state on the other. Liberal principles are generally formulated in a negative way, in terms of freedom 'from' (mostly from state intervention), whereas social rights are formulated in a positive way; they imply an active and even interventionist state. These social rights are meant to give the *formal* status of citizenship a *material* foundation. A certain level of material well-being is guaranteed, which enables the citizen to exercise his or her rights to full participation in the community. This implies that, in the perception of Marshall, social citizenship marks the 'end of history' or at least 'the end of the history of citizenship'.

An intriguing question is, now, how do we look at this in our own time, more than forty years after Marshall developed his ideas. It will become evident that in this book, the notion of social citizenship as the *final* stage is not accepted. On the contrary, certain new types of citizenship are unfolded in the light of new developments and problems with which we are confronted today. We can mention in this respect: the notion of neo-republican citizenship (van Gunsteren, Chapter 4), of cultural citizenship (Turner, Chapter 12), of active citizenship (Adriaansens, Chapter 6), of race-neutral and gender-neutral citizenship (Wilson, Chapter 5; Vogel, Chapter 7), of global citizenship (Falk, Chapter 10), of European citizenship (Habermas, Chapter 3) and of ecological citizenship (van Steenbergen, Chapter 11).

A second point of difference is that Marshall was optimistic that the introduction of social citizenship would not only mean the final, but also the 'crowning stage' (Fraser and Gordon, Chapter 8) in the historical development of citizenship and he did not take into account the possibility of a setback. Here it becomes very clear that new developments and problems, especially since the 1980s, have put pressure on these notions of citizenship. Social citizenship, in particular, is under fire.

This means, in short, that the contributions to this book reflect two tendencies: the use of the Marshallian concepts of citizenship as still valuable tools to analyse and 'solve' a number of the problems of the 1990s, on the one hand, and the development of new concepts of citizenship (which also could be described as extensions of the old concepts) to tackle those problems of present day society, which cannot be analysed or solved within the framework of the classic aspects of citizenship: civil, political and social.

Although we are dealing here with a great variety of problems and questions, both of these tendencies also encompass one key issue or problem. When dealing with the more classic use of citizenship, the problem of *inclusion* and *exclusion* plays a crucial role. It is an old problem, but it has gained momentum over the past few years with the emergence of the new underclass, the emancipation of minority groups, the attacks on the welfare state and the questions surrounding participation and marginalization.

When dealing with the extension or renewal of the concept of citizenship, it is *internationalization* which plays the encompassing role. Marshall has often been criticized for being too British. He did not take into account that the development of citizenship might be different in other societies and, what is even more important here, he did not explore the possibility of citizenship in a broader context than the national one.

Inclusion and exclusion

Several authors in this volume deal with the question of inclusion and exclusion, of first- and second-class citizenship. The notion of the *new underclass* has emerged over the past few years. It should be emphasized, however, that we are not dealing here with a 'class' in the Marxian sense of the term; and it might be better to use the term second-class citizens.

The first difference with the nineteenth century of Karl Marx is that we are dealing here with a *minority*. The so-called 'two-thirds society' indicates that there is a great majority which is well off, whereas until deep into the twentieth century the lower classes constituted a majority in society. More important is a second difference; this underclass cannot present a threat, for it has no power to change the economic system; on the contrary, as Dahrendorf (Chapter 2) points out, its members are politically harmless and economically superfluous. Therefore they do not form much of a problem, neither politically nor economically. Tolerating the existence of such an underclass, however, betrays the basic values of citizenship. Therefore, its mere existence poses a challenge to the moral foundations of our society.

This underclass may be 'only' a minority in modern Western societies; it is nevertheless a sizeable minority and, what is worse, its membership is rapidly growing, especially in the United States. William Julius Wilson, the 'inventor' of the underclass concept, gives us a grim picture of its situation there (see Chapter 5). In particular, the circumstances of the inner-city ghetto poor have deteriorated since the early 1970s, when Johnson launched his 'Great Society'.

In this context it is not surprising that in the United States a rich elaborated discourse on *civil* citizenship is combined with a near-total absence of debate about *social* citizenship, as Fraser and Gordon point out (Chapter 8). According to them, the emphasis on civil and political *rights*, on the one hand, and social *obligations*, on the other, is mainly caused by the property-related aspect of civil citizenship, which creates the greatest obstacle to the building of social citizenship. The situation in most European welfare states looks less ferocious but Wilson warns that the opening-up of national borders, the expected stream of immigrants from Eastern Europe and Northern Africa and the decreased need for unskilled workers may lead to a similar concentration of members of the underclass in the big cities of Europe.

Nevertheless, up to now the situation in Europe has been better than in the United States, at least as far as sheer poverty is concerned, and in that sense the underclass cannot be compared with the nineteenth-century *Lumpenproletariat*. But of greater concern than actual poverty is the social isolation and marginaliza-tion of the underclass. The social security systems make it possible that members of this underclass are able to survive *physically*, but perhaps not *socially*, in the sense that they are separated from the main stream of society, and the required characteristics of 'good' citizenship, such as autonomy, self-reliance and participation in the community, are not applicable here.

What is at stake is the *quality* of life or, in the context of this book, the quality of citizenship, and this affects much broader layers of the population. In particular Adriaansens (Chapter 6) shows that we are dealing here with a problem which does not only affect the underclass. Citizenship means primarily social participation and integration and the best way to achieve this goal is to increase the level of labour participation, since work may prove to be the most important integrating factor in society, especially since so many traditional institutions of social cohesion, like the Church and the local community, have been eroded in recent decades.

Adriaansens makes a plea for a social policy which improves the labour participation of the population. Wilson (Chapter 5) does something similar, but he adds that such a policy should be *race-neutral* and not only include job skill programmes and similar things, but also an improvement in public education and health care. Somewhat in line with Wilson, but of a more theoretical nature, are the proposals of Vogel for *gender-neutral* citizenship.

She emphasizes that women have not been altogether excluded from the story of citizenship. They have been part of it, but as subjects and subordinates of citizens. Women, and particularly married women, were included within an institutional framework of *Herrschaft* and subordination that was itself part of a wider culture of citizenship. Although marriage is today no longer a (legal) site of domination and subordination, it is still the case that women's full participation in the rights and obligations of citizenship is considerably impeded by the 'vulnerability of marriage'.

Even more than in Western societies, the concepts of citizenship and civil society are topical in the countries of Central and Eastern Europe. It seems that they are seen as the antithesis of everything that has to do with the old regime – the corrupt state bureaucracy, the totalitarian party, the passive and docile population – and for this reason they have an enormous appeal. In post-Communist society people prefer to see themselves as citizens and no longer as comrades.

According to Agh (Chapter 9), the intelligentsia is playing a central role in this transition process. Since Eastern Europe consists of strongly fragmented societies, the intelligentsia has functioned there as a 'replacement class' for citizens. This has had its influence on the way citizenship and civil society have been defined in that region. Agh is very critical of this transition process, since it has led to a replacement of an 'elite-autocracy' by an 'elite-democracy' as the masses did not play any role in these revolutions. There are, however, signs of a breakthrough in the form of a citizens-awakening, a building of a civil society, based on self-defence against the state.

Internationalization

All modern societies are coping with the process of internationalization; a process which is especially important for us, since citizenship has been historically bound to the nation-state, as Habermas points out in Chapter 3. He adds, however, that citizenship was never conceptually tied to national identity and some vision of a world civil society was already developed by Immanuel Kant.

Here, four notions of expanding citizenship as an outcome of internationalization are discussed. To start with there is the burning question of European citizenship. Habermas (Chapter 3) considers the question of whether there will ever be such a thing as European citizenship, and he means by this not only the possibilities for collective political action across national borders, but also the consciousness of an obligation towards the European common weal. It is interesting that as late as 1974 Raymond Aron answered this question with a resolute 'no'. Nowadays the situation seems to be different; Eurosclerosis has vanished and the notion of a citizens' Europe has gained popularity. The present anti-European tendencies may be more against the Europe of Eurocrats and multi-nationals than against the unification of Europe as such.

Habermas seems to be rather optimistic about the possibilities of a European citizenship. Examples of multicultural societies like Switzerland and the United States demonstrate that a political culture by no means has to be based on all citizens sharing the same language or the same ethnic and cultural origins. Rather the political culture must serve as the common denominator for a constitutional patriotism. This sharpens an awareness of the multiplicity and integrity of different forms of life which coexist in a multicultural society. According to Habermas, a future federal Republic of European States should follow a model of balancing between universalism and particularism. Both he and Dahrendorf (Chapter 2) are of the opinion that a heterogeneous European commonwealth would be a step in the right direction, but that an 'Europe des regions' would be a bad formula.

A possible (and for many logical) next step in this process of internationalization is globalization. Falk (Chapter 10) has gone deeply into the question of the meaning of global citizenship. He has his doubts whether this is the next logical step or, in other words, whether there is a sort of historical trajectory from the city via the nation-state and the region to the globe. In his opinion, the recent process of Europeanization has led to a form of inward-looking and to a tendency to ignore the world beyond Europe, sustaining a relatively insular posture towards contemporary world history.

The notion of global citizenship is not univocal; on the contrary, Falk distinguishes no less than five partly overlapping, but also contradictory, images of global citizenship: the global reformer; the elite global businessman; the manager of the world order in the light of environmental problems; the rise of the politically conscious regionalist (which may or may not be a step towards globalism); and the emergent transnational activist.

This means that the overall project of global citizenship needs to be understood as a series of projects and that global citizenship becomes essentially a normative undertaking, since some of the above images would fit better than others in a perspective of global community as Falk envisages it, based on social responsibility, solidarity, a feeling for equity and for nature.

Internationalization of citizenship should not necessarily refer to territorial extension. The emphasis can be on one aspect which is inherently international. In this book we are confronted with two other new notions of citizenship, which can be described as *ecological* and *cultural* and which are global in scope. From its very beginning in the late 1960s and early 1970s (one can think in this respect of the first Report to the Club of Rome: 'Limits to growth'), the so-called environmental *'problematique'* was seen as a problem of the planet as a whole; and the United Nations Conference of June 1992 in Rio de Janeiro confirmed this once more.

In this volume at least three authors discuss ecological problems in connection with world citizenship. Dahrendorf (Chapter 2) defines it as a question of human habitat, and in this context he stresses that citizenship can never be complete until it is world citizenship. His main concern is whether the necessity to move to a liveable environment, and thus to sustainable development, can be accomplished without violating certain entitlements of citizenship which seem to be linked to economic expansion. In short, can we survive in freedom? For Dahrendorf, it is freedom that matters above all, even above survival.

In Falk's typology of global citizens (Chapter 10) we find two types which in one way or another are concerned with environmental problems. The first type is managerial: the environment is in danger, but is also a challenge for politicians and industrialists. The second type is the environmental activist as part of transactional activism, which manifests itself also in other fields like women's, peace and Third World issues.

In Chapter 11, I also make a distinction between two types of global environmental citizens: first, there is the *earth citizen*, who is aware of his or her organic process of birth and growth out of the earth as a living organism (the earth as Gaia). The two key concepts here are *care* (as distinct from control) and humans as *participants in nature* (as distinct from humans as rulers and subjugators of nature). These last characteristics can be found in the second type of global environmental citizen, who can be described as the *world citizen*, for whom the environment is 'big science' and the planet an object of global management, which requires large scale organization and big government.

The last type of extension of citizenship is developed by Turner (Chapter 12). Originally, citizenship was limited to the realm of politics and economics. In our century Marshall added the social dimension and now Turner begs attention for a *cultural* dimension. Cultural citizenship, according to him, consists in those social practices which enable a competent citizen to participate fully in the national culture. Educational institutions, especially universities, are thus crucial to cultural citizenship, because they are an essential aspect of the socialization of the child into a national system of values.

It is remarkable that Turner uses the adjective 'national' twice here. This is probably because he describes cultural citizenship in general terms as a phenomenon of the modern era. However, crucial for the most recent developments of cultural citizenship is the *globalization of culture*, which can be associated with the growing interconnectedness of the world economy and the development of a world market in cultural goods. Globalization of culture also involves the idea of societies conceptualizing themselves as part of a world system of societies, as part of a global order.

This process of cultural globalization has two characteristics, which Turner describes as 'democratization' and 'postmodernization'. By this last process Turner means an increasing fragmentation and differentiation of culture as a consequence of the plurality of life-styles and the differentiation of social structure. In short, it is the celebration of the idea of difference and heterogeneity against sameness and standardization. Turner expresses some hope that these processes will prevent recent tendencies towards (new forms of) exclusion.

As will by now be apparent, the book can be divided into three parts. The first part deals with general questions of citizenship as found in the contributions of Dahrendorf, Habermas and van Gunsteren (Chapters 2–4). The second part concerns inclusion and exclusion. This part consists of the articles by Wilson, Adriaansens, Vogel, Fraser/Gordon and Agh (Chapters 5–9). The third part deals with the question of internationalization of citizenship. The contributions by Falk, van Steenbergen and Turner (Chapters 10–12) can be found here. Most of the contributions in this volume are based on papers presented at the Conference on the Quality of Citizenship which took place at Utrecht/Zeist (The Netherlands) in March 1991 and which was organized by the Department of General Social Sciences of the University of Utrecht.

2

THE CHANGING QUALITY OF CITIZENSHIP

Ralf Dahrendorf

Who now speaks of the limits to growth? Some 'evergreens' do and remind us of the risks which threaten modern societies; but even they are concerned more with the need to limit growth than with its God-given limits. We know that our planet could not sustain American per capita GNP for Chinese and Indians, or even one of the two; but then no one expects this contingency to occur within relevant time. In any case, we seem to have reconciled in our minds the constraints of the human habitat and the desires of greedy humans; we solemnly declare that ecology and economy are not or need not be in conflict, and carry on with growth. Small is beautiful? Never has bigness been more fashionable than in these years of mergers and takeovers. The year 1973 and all that is forgotten. After twenty-four hours of the second phase of the Gulf War it became clear that the oil price would fall rather than rise, and that business could, therefore, continue as usual.

The experience of the last decades

Yet it is worth looking more closely at the experience of the 1970s and 1980s. Jürgen Habermas used a word of interesting ambiguity when he called this period, *unübersichtlich*, and even spoke of a *neue Unübersichtlichkeit*.[1] The ambiguity lies in the notion that things are both opaque and resistant to the observer who wants to survey them; our inability to make sense of them reflects an objective difficulty. I shall argue that the course of the past two decades is in fact fairly clear. It contains a lesson and a question, and both have to do with the subject of this volume: citizenship and its quality.

Ten years ago, a book was written entitled *The Rise and Decline of Nations*.[2] Its author, the economist Mancur Olson, was unlucky. When his book appeared in 1982 its central thesis was about to be falsified. This central thesis has to do with the logic of collective action: given a sufficiently long period of sociopolitical stability (so Olson argued), the cartel of special interests will lead economies into stagflation. Social rigidities are bound to produce a combination of high expectations and shrinking capacity to satisfy them; hence inflation and low or no growth. Almost all OECD countries have had the experience; some are presently going through a reminder of its aches and pains. Olson was doubtful about the prospects of changing this condition from within. In the United States, it was possible to leave the declining north-east and go west and south, but in Europe there is no such opportunity. Olson gets quite carried away by this depressing prospect and writes that it makes us 'appreciate anew Thomas Jefferson's observation that "the tree of liberty must be refreshed from time to time with the blood of patriots and tyrants"'.[3] It takes wars or revolutions to break up the rigidities of stagflation.

In fact, all it took was Margaret Thatcher and Ronald Reagan. The supply-side turn of the 1980s is not easily explained. I doubt whether its most prominent protagonists, let alone Felipe Gonzales in Spain, or Bob Hawke and David Lange in Australia and New Zealand, or even François Mitterrand Deux after 1982–3 had read Friedrich von Hayek, Milton Friedman, the public choice theorists at the University of Virginia, or the authors and editors of *Commentary* magazine. Change was in the air, and this change gave clear signals. The burden of the welfare state weighed heavily on many. In the end, a lot of people got back from the state what they had paid to its treasury in taxes, minus the cost of public bureaucracies. This condition stymied the motivation of most, and above all the Schumpeterian sense of entrepreneurship by creative destructiveness. Something had to be done. Public expenditure had to be cut, and taxes with it. People, business people above all, had to be helped back on to their own feet and encouraged to start running. One day, the economic history of the 1980s will be written. Then, we shall remember that earlier Thatcher, the French first minister of the 1830s and 1840s, François Guizot, who coined a phrase: *enrichissez-vous, messieurs!* Get rich quick, and if you can't, get a loan, borrow! The casino capitalism of the 1980s was also capitalism on credit. Still, it produced seven years of unrivalled growth in the OECD world.

It also produced a general loosening-up of socioeconomic structures which had become rigid. The process affected not just OECD countries but those of the Comecon world as well. In my *Reflections on the Revolution in Europe* I argued that the 1980s differed in important respects from the 1950s and 1960s.[4] During the earlier period, the First World grew quickly and the Second World slowly, but both grew. During the 1980s, one grew whereas the other stagnated and even declined. An increasingly greedy *nomenklatura* exploited its subjects who were already disadvantaged and who also could not fail to notice what went on next door to them in the West. Thus the *ancien regime* syndrome was aggravated by travel and television. All it took was a spark to set the powder keg on fire. The spark had a name, Gorbachev. The revolution of 1989 ensued.

Provisions and entitlements

The end of history? It takes a very blinkered mind to put about such an idea. In fact, many of us feel that history is very much on the move; we get almost dizzy with its pace. History, says Popper, has no meaning, but we must try to give it meaning.[5] We can do so as moral beings, and also as scholars; we can act, and we can understand. It helps us to understand the events of the past decade if we think of modern politics as being about two great themes. One has to do with growth, with widening the range of choices, with the supply side or, as I shall call it, with *provisions*. The other theme has to do with access to the many choices on offer, with opportunities, entry tickets, effective demand, with *entitlements*. The two need not be in conflict. Great political movements, like that of the early liberal bourgeoisie, and great authors, like John Maynard Keynes, have managed to combine them for their own time. But, in theory, the tension between economics and politics will never be resolved, however hopefully we invoke the notion of political economy, and, in practice, provisions and entitlements are usually the core concerns of different and often antagonistic parties. Certainly, the 1980s were a decade of growing provisions in which many entitlements, not just those of the welfare state, fell by the wayside.

Before I continue the story, let me say that citizenship belongs squarely on the entitlement side of this picture. The point is important. It is no doubt a sign of the times – that is, of the open questions at the end of the 1980s boom – that citizenship has become a fashionable concept all over the political spectrum. People sense that there is something in citizenship that defines the needs of the future – in this they are right – but proceed to bend the term to their own predilections. The right prefers to speak of 'active citizenship' in order to emphasize the obligations of people.[6] The left tries to develop a notion of 'communitarian citizenship' which combines solidarity with welfare rights.[7] The centre turns the concept into an almost vacuous label for everything that is not to be regarded as either right or left. At times one wants to despair at the distortions of one of the great ideas of social and political thought, and begins to wonder whether it can be rescued from its ideological abuses. But it must be.

Many, myself included, think of T.H. Marshall's *Citizenship and Social Class* as a key text for understanding the concept.[8] Marshall defines citizenship as the body of rights and duties – the status – which goes with full membership of a society. This status is by definition removed from the vagaries of the market. Citizenship is a non-economic concept. It defines people's standing independent of the relative value attached to their contribution to the economic process. The elements of citizenship are thus unconditional. This is as true for obligations as it is for rights. The right to vote, for example, is not dependent on paying taxes, although paying taxes is an obligation associated with the status of citizenship.

The point is important and topical. The British debate about a 'poll tax' (technically the 'community charge') is a case in point. In some of its protagonists' minds, it reverses an old principle and stipulates that there should be 'no representation without taxation'; people should not be allowed to vote for local authorities for which they do not pay. Similarly, the American concept of 'workfare' links welfare rights to people's readiness to work. Both are examples of the excesses of the provisions decade. Rights are dissolved into marketable commodities; they are offered for sale. Lawrence Mead has turned this approach, in his book, *Beyond Entitlements*, into a theory of sorts, which does not make it any more plausible.[9] There may be a case for emphasizing obligations as well as rights, even for a more sparing definition of citizenship rights, but once they lose their unconditional quality, the door is open not just for the invisible hand of the market (which can be benevolent), but above all for the visible hand of rulers who tell people what to do when. Thus the poll tax is turned into effective disenfranchisement and workfare into forms of forced labour.

T.H. Marshall is also quoted by many, myself included, for his description of the gradual extension of citizenship rights from the civil to the political and further to the social sphere. The time may well have come to look again at the way in which Marshall sets up his argument. I wonder whether it might not be better to think of the rights of citizenship as a pattern of concentric circles. There is a hard core of fundamental and indispensable rights: the integrity of the person, due process of law, freedom of speech and other rights of expression. The canon of basic human rights without which the rule of law becomes an empty shell belongs here. These fundamental rights are under all circumstances important. However, basic human and civil rights have too little meaning for people who for reasons outside their control are unable to make use of them. They therefore lead to a series of needs of empowerment which may also acquire the quality of rights.

What should or should not be included in these enabling rights is a legitimate subject of debate, and of political struggles. Most would agree today that the right to vote is a necessary corollary of civil status. Legal aid for those who cannot afford to take legal action is a prerequisite of the due process of law. As one pursues the argument one will soon enter T.H. Marshall's proper territory, that is, modern social policy and the entitlements which it conveys. However, there are familiar yet crucial questions. How much of people's social status should be removed from the vagaries of the market? Is there any plausible and practicable way of drawing the line between equality of opportunity and equality of results? Are there perhaps acceptable and unacceptable ways of delivering social entitlements of citizenship with, say, basic income guarantees at one end and a plethora of welfare state bureaucracies at the other? The territory is familiar; it covers the well-trodden ground of liberty and equality, or of justice in a free society: how and to what extent does the core of human and civil rights need to be backed up by a secondary set of lesser, but none the less critical, entitlements? We know Hayek's answer, and we think we know that of Rawls, but I am not sure that we have a clear sense either in theory or in practice of how to define the constitution of liberty. Indeed, perhaps different times require different answers.

Let me leave such conceptual matters for the moment and return to social analysis. The 1980s, or at any rate the years following the recession at their beginning, were a decade of economic growth, and thus of provisions, in the OECD world. They were also a decade that saw a loosening up of rigidities everywhere. At the beginning of the 1990s there are signs of change. We may well see a new emphasis on entitlements. I want to allude to three major reasons for such a change of direction, one relating to the West, one to the post-Communist East, and one to global concerns.

The new underclass

I said that entitlements fell by the wayside during the provisions decade of the 1980s. The most tangible effect of this process is the emergence of an underclass in most of the rich societies of the OECD world. These are people – long-term unemployed, persistent poor, disadvantaged ethnic groups, or all of these and more – who have fallen through the net. They have lost regular and guaranteed access to markets, especially the labour market, to the political community, to networks of legitimate social relations. William Julius Wilson has, more than anyone, helped us understand this category, though it is not always what he calls, a 'ghetto under-class'.[10] It varies in size, composition and, above all, in the extent to which it has become a hardened social category or remained one from which people find it possible and desirable to escape. The question which I want to raise here is, however, another one; it is less obvious than it may sound: why is the underclass a problem? If we knew the answer, we would also have the beginnings of a solution.

The underclass does not pose a class problem. Technically, the name, under*class*, is wrong. Classes are conflict groups based on common interest conditions within a framework of relations. They need each other, and their members are needed. They therefore carry their solutions within them, as it were. Over time, class conflicts remove their own foundation. Today, industrial labour – or what is left of it – is very much within the majority class of those who have an interest in preserving the status quo. The underclass on the contrary is a mere category, a victim. It is unlikely to organize and defend the many similar yet not really common interests of its members. They are, if the cruelty of the statement is pardonable, not needed. The rest could and would quite like to live without them. Thus they cannot help themselves, except as individuals. They need catalysts and outside agents, or else changes in prevailing values.

The underclass does not pose an ordinary status problem either. It does not simply comprise those at the bottom of the ladder of social stratification. The point is, rather, that its members cannot even get their feet on the first rung of the ladder. Measures of redistribution, for what they are worth, do not reach this category. The universe of stratification is a universe of gradations and of mobility: the position of the underclass is one beyond the threshold of basic opportunities of access. It is a problem of entitlements, and thus of citizenship.

It therefore touches the basic values – in that sense, the moral texture – of our societies. Tolerating an underclass is economically feasible and politically riskless. But it betrays a readiness to suspend the basic values of citizenship – equal rights of participation for all – for one category of people, which by the same token weakens the intrinsically universal claims of these values. Differently put, if we allow say 5 per cent to be denied access to our civic community, we should not be surprised if doubts about the validity of our values spread throughout the social fabric. In this sense, evident problems of law and order are at least indirectly a consequence of underclass exclusion.[11] The majority will pay a high price for turning away from those who consistently fail to make it, and the fact that the price is initially moral rather than economic should not deceive anyone about its seriousness.

Incidentally, and as a footnote to the argument though not to our predicament, there is a deep similarity between the underclass problem in rich countries and the problem of the poor countries – the so-called LDCs or less-developed countries – on a world scale. They too are economically 'not needed' and politically harmless, but challenge our moral foundations. In due course they will force us to realize that citizenship is either a universal project or a miserable cloak for privilege.

Self-determination and the position of minorities

This takes me to the second set of pressures for a revival of interest in the entitlements of citizenship. For many in the formerly Communist countries of East Central Europe and elsewhere it sounds almost cynical to call the decade of the 1980s one of provisions. Provisions, choices, economic and otherwise, are exactly what they did not have then and want to have now. But they are beginning to realize that even a functioning economy requires citizens. Participation in markets is not a matter of course. The seemingly simple legal prerequisites of freedom of contract and reliable titles to private property constitute major stumbling blocks on the road to expanding provisions. When I called the early liberal bourgeoisie a great movement what I had in mind was precisely its effective interest in both basic civil rights and conditions of economic growth. There is no such group in the post-Communist countries.

The result is confusion, despair and the search for certainties to which people hope to cling. Citizenship in these circumstances becomes less an entitlement than a definition. People want to know where they belong, and they want to belong to familiar and homogeneous groups, not to a Czech and Slovak Federal Republic, but to Slovakia, and perhaps to the Hungarian ethnic group within it. There are many explanations for this process other than economic and political despair, but the effect is a shift from issues of the substance of civic entitlements to boundary questions. The result is deplorable. In the name of self-determination, the prospects of citizenship are put at risk.

It is tempting to think of citizenship as blossoming in communities which are not riven by ethnic strife or religious division, but it is also wrong. The true test of the strength of citizenship rights is heterogeneity. Common respect for basic entitlements among people who are different in origin, culture and creed proves that combination of identity and variety which lies at the heart of civil and civilized societies. The treatment of minorities is crucial, and it raises serious questions in those regions which are most vociferous about self-determination. If their national leaders succeed, they often begin with banning minority languages and end with persecuting or expelling those who are different. The refugee, that characteristic social figure of our time, is the victim of intolerant homogeneity, and is therefore the greatest and saddest expression of the need for real citizenship.

Where does it blossom if not in homogeneous self-determining nations? For the time being, and paradoxically perhaps, the answer must be: in heterogeneous nation-states. Note the difference: nations are tribes of equals, but nation-states are deliberate constructions for the common good. So far as organized human communities go, the heterogeneous nation-state under the rule of law and equipped with democratic institutions is the greatest constitutional achievement of history. It is not the last word; but it is the best one for the time being. Europe, by which I mean the European Community, has so far signally failed to provide rights of citizenship on a wider scale. Perhaps it should; the Spanish government in particular has pressed for such extensions recently, and great individuals like Jean Monnet and Altiero Spinelli have done so in the past, but so far the Community is centred around provisions rather than entitlements, it is an *economic* community. No one should lightly abandon the guarantees of citizenship which civilized nation-states offer for the promises of prosperity in a large single market. And the worst formula of all is that of an *Europe des regions* which takes us back to the tribes on the one hand, and forward to provisions without entitlements on the other.

These may be shocking statements to some, and they clearly need to be substantiated. Perhaps it helps if I add that citizenship is never complete until it is world citizenship. Exclusion is the enemy of citizenship. A heterogeneous European commonwealth of law might indeed be a stepping stone in the right direction. (The Council of Europe has its important place for this very reason.) But at the end of the road there must be Immanuel Kant's vision of a world civil society.[12]

Can we survive in freedom?

This is all the more important in view of the third major pressure for remembering the power of citizenship in the 1990s. Many attempts have been made to use this power for adding weight to political demands. Instead of initiating a campaign against poverty, people call poverty a violation of human rights. Instead of trying to abolish unemployment, they stipulate a right to work. Are judges supposed to do the work of politicians? Such confused thinking helps no one and serves to dilute the notion of entitlements as a part of the basic status of membership in a community. There is, however, one set of issues which may need to be thought of as a part of the penumbra of citizenship; it has to do with the risks which threaten human life on our planet. I am not sure whether one can stipulate an entitlement for all of us as world citizens to a liveable habitat, and thus to actions which sustain it, but something of this kind may well belong on the agenda of citizenship.

The notion has its difficulties. The core of human and civil rights can be, and has been, clearly defined. Certain political institutions to back up this core – the constitution of liberty in the strict sense – are widely accepted. Their characteristic is that they provide chances rather than determining objectives; they are in that sense formal rules of the game. As we move to the social and economic entitlements which back up basic citizenship rights, the question of formal rules versus substantive interventions is precisely the issue. I would argue that those entitlements are preferable which give opportunities rather than prescribe a particular path to people. Basic income guarantees are preferable to child benefits, housing benefits and means-tested social security payments. Moreover, the tax system is a better vehicle for delivering guarantees than any specific bureaucracy. As we move on to a liveable environment and thus to sustainable growth, an even more difficult question arises. It is that of how we can curb unfettered expansion without violating other entitlements of citizenship. Can we survive in freedom? This may well be the most significant question before us, and I am not at all sure about the answer.[13] For those who share my own belief that freedom matters above all – even above survival – the alternative is literally vital.

I started this chapter on a somewhat flippant note. It is hard to speak about the 1980s other than in their own terms. But I cannot finish in the same way, because the party is over. In the 1990s we are faced with more than economic issues, and activating the supply side will only take us a little further. Most major questions require attention to entitlements. The underclass, national self-determination and the human habitat are three important issues in themselves and, at the same time, symptoms of today's and tomorrow's needs. We are approaching another millennium. There is something ridiculously arbitrary – and, of course, culture-bound – about the year 2000, but no doubt it will encourage a whole lot of Reverend Joneses to engage in fundamentalist and ultimately suicidal nonsense. Disorientated people, and there are many everywhere, will succumb and allow themselves to be lured to the killing fields by them. The open society is no guarantee against such risks, but it is the only answer which we have got if we want to survive in freedom. Citizenship rights are at the heart of the open society. They need to be reformulated by precise minds who do not use them for devious ends or to cloak vested interests. They need to be reasserted by those who recognize that reform is the only hope of liberty. And they need to be extended to cope with new challenges. Who said that there is no longer an agenda for change?

Notes

1 Jürgen Habermas, *Die Neue Unübersichtlichkeit* (Suhrkamp, Frankfurt, 1985).

2 Mancur Olson, *The Rise and Decline of Nations* (Yale University Press, New Haven and London, 1982).

3 Ibid., p. 141.

4 Ralf Dahrendorf, *Reflections on the Revolution in Europe* (Chatto/Random House, London/New York, 1990).

5. Karl R. Popper, *The Open Society and its Enemies* (Routledge & Kegan Paul, London, 1952), p. 269.

6 See *Encouraging Citizenship*. Report of the Commission on Citizenship (HMSO, London, 1990).

7 See R. Plant and others in Geoff Andress (ed.), *Citizenship* (Lawrence & Wishart, London, 1991).

8 Thomas H. Marshall, *Citizenship and Social Class* (Cambridge University Press, Cambridge, 1950).

9 Lawrence Mead, *Beyond Entitlement: the Social Obligations of Citizenship* (Free Press, New York, 1986).

10 More recently, Wilson himself has preferred another description *The Truly Disadvantaged* (University of Chicago Press, Chicago, 1987). See also his contribution in Chapter 5 of this volume.

11 I have argued this case in some detail in *Law and Order* (Stevens & Sons, London, 1985).

12 Kant's short 'popular essays', and notably the 'Idea for a universal history with cosmopolitan intent', remain topical.

13 Ulrich Beck is a sociologist who has a sense of this *problematique*; his *Die Risikogesellschaft* (Suhrkamp, Frankfurt, 1986) and *Politik in der Risikogesellschaft* (Suhrkamp, Frankfurt, 1991).

3

CITIZENSHIP AND NATIONAL IDENTITY

Jürgen Habermas

Up to the middle of the 1980s history seemed to be gradually entering that crystalline state known as *posthistoire*, to use Arnold Gehlen's term for the strange feeling that *tout se change mais rien ne va plus*. In the iron grip of systemic constraints all possibilities seemed to have been exhausted, all alternatives frozen dead, and all avenues still open to have become meaningless. This mood has changed in the mean time. History has become mobilized, it is accelerating, even overheating. The new problems are shifting old perspectives and, what is more important, opening up new perspectives for the future, points of view that restore our ability to perceive alternative courses of action.

Two historical movements of a contemporary history that is once again in flux touch upon the relation between citizenship and national identity. First, the issue of the future of the nation-state has unexpectedly become topical in the wake of German reunification, the liberation of the Central Eastern European states and the ethnic conflicts that are breaking out throughout Eastern Europe. Secondly, the fact that the states of the European Community are gradually growing together, especially with the impending caesura which will be created by the introduction of the currency union, sheds some light on the relaxation between nation-state and democracy, for the democratic processes that have gone hand in hand with the nation-state lag hopelessly behind the supranational form taken by economic integration.

These topics offer an occasion for a conceptual clarification of some of the normative standpoints from which we will, I hope, be able to sharpen our understanding of the complex relation between citizenship and national identity.

The role of nationalism

Recent events in Germany and Eastern Europe have given a new twist to discussion in Germany of the gradual development of postnational society.[1] Many German intellectuals have complained of the democratic deficit incurred by a process of unification that has been effected more at an administrative and economic level than by enlisting the participation of its citizens; they now find themselves accused of 'postnational arrogance'. The controversy as to the form and speed of unification has not only been fuelled by contradictory feelings, but also by confusing thoughts and concepts. One side conceived of the five new states' joining the Federal Republic as restoring the unity of a nation-state torn apart four decades ago. From this viewpoint, the nation constitutes the pre-political unity of a community with a shared common historical destiny. The other side conceived of the political unification as restoring democracy and a constitutional state in a territory where civil rights had been suspended in one form or another since 1933. From this viewpoint, what used to be West Germany was no less a nation of citizens than is the new Federal Republic. With this republican usage, the term 'nation-state' is stripped of precisely those pre-political connotations with which the expression was laden in modern Europe. Loosening the semantic connections between national citizenship and national identity takes into account that the classic form of the nation-state is at present disintegrating. This is confirmed by a glance back at its rise in early modern times.

In modern Europe the premodern form of the *empire* which used to unite numerous peoples remained rather unstable, as in the cases of the Holy Roman Empire or the Russian and Ottoman empires. A different, federal form of state emerged from the belt of Central European cities in what was formerly Lorraine, the heart of the Carolingian Empire. It was in Switzerland that a *federation* sprang up strong enough to balance the ethnic tensions within a multicultural association of citizens. However, it was only the *territorial states* with a central administration that exerted a structuring influence on the system of European states. In the sixteenth century, kingdoms gave birth to those territorial states – such as England, France, Portugal, Spain and Sweden – which were later on, in the course of democratization in line with the French example, gradually transformed into *nation-states*.[2] This state formation secured the overall conditions in which capitalism was then able to develop worldwide. The nation-state provided both the infrastructure for rational administration and the legal frame for free individual and collective action. Moreover, and it is this which shall interest us here, the nation-state laid the foundations for cultural and ethnic homogeneity on the basis of which it then proved possible to push ahead with the democratization of government from the late eighteenth century, although this was achieved at the cost of excluding ethnic minorities. The nation-state and democracy are the twins born of the French Revolution. From a cultural point of view, both have been growing in the shadow of *nationalism*.

Nationalism is the term for a specifically modern phenomenon of cultural integration. This type of national consciousness is formed in social movements and emerges from modernization processes at a time when people are at once both mobilized and isolated as individuals. Nationalism is a form of collective consciousness which both presupposes a reflexive appropriation of cultural traditions that has been filtered through historiography and spreads only via the channels of modern mass communication. Both elements lend nationalism the artificial traits of something that is to a certain extent a construct, thus rendering it by definition susceptible to manipulative misuse by political elites.

The history of the term 'nation' mirrors in a peculiar way the emergence of the nation-state.[3] For the Romans, *natio* was the goddess of birth and origin. *Natio* referred, like *gens* and *populus* and unlike *civitas*, to peoples and tribes who were not yet organized in political associations; indeed, the Romans often referred to 'savage', 'barbaric' or 'pagan' peoples. In this classic usage, therefore, nations are communities of people of the same descent, who are integrated geographically in the form of settlements or neighbourhoods, and culturally by their common language, customs and traditions, but who are not yet politically integrated in the form of state organization. This meaning persisted throughout the Middle Ages and indeed in early modern times. Even Kant still maintained that 'that group which recognizes itself as being gathered together in a society due to common descent shall be called a nation (gens)'. Yet since the middle of the eighteenth century, the differences in meaning between 'nation' and '*Staatsvolk*', that is 'nation' and 'politically organized people', have gradually been disappearing. With the French Revolution the nation even became the source of state sovereignty, e.g. in the thought of Sieyès. Each nation is now supposed to be granted the right of political self-determination. Indeed, in the nineteenth century the conservative representatives of the German Historical School equated the principle of nationality with the 'principle of revolution'.

The meaning of the term 'nation' thus changed from designating a pre-political entity to something that was supposed to play a constitutive role in defining the political identity of the citizen within a democratic polity. In the final instance, the manner in which national identity determines citizenship can in fact be reversed. Thus the gist of Ernest Renan's famous saying that *'l'existence d'une nation est . . . plébiscite de tous les jours'* is already directed *against* nationalism. After 1871, Renan was only able to counter the German Empire's claims to the Alsace by referring to the inhabitants' French nationality because he could conceive of the 'nation' as a nation of citizens. The nation of citizens does not derive its identity from common ethnic and cultural properties but rather from the praxis of citizens who actively exercise their civil rights. At this juncture, the republican strand of 'citizenship' parts company completely from the idea of belonging to a pre-political community integrated on the basis of descent, a shared tradition and a common language. Viewed from this end, the initial fusion of republicanism with nationalism only functioned as a catalyst.

That nationalism which was inspired by the works of historians and romantic writers founded a collective identity that played a *functional* role in the implementation of citizenship that arose in the French Revolution. In the melting-pot of national consciousness, the ascriptive features of one's origin were now transformed into just as many achieved properties, resulting from a reflexive appropriation of tradition. Hereditary nationality gave way to an acquired nationalism, that is a product of one's own conscious striving. This nationalism was able to foster people's identification with a role which demanded a high degree of personal commitment, even to the point of self-sacrifice: in this respect, general conscription was only the other side of the civil rights coin. Nationalism and republicanism combined in the willingness to fight and if necessary die for one's country. This explains the complementary relation of mutual reinforcement that originally obtained between nationalism and republicanism, the one becoming the vehicle for the emergence of the other.

However, this sociopsychological connection does not mean to say that the two are linked in conceptual terms. Compare 'freedom' in the sense of national independence, that is, collective self-assertion *vis-à-vis* other nations, with 'freedom' in the sense of those political liberties the individual citizen enjoys within a country; the two notions are so different in meaning that at a later point the modern understanding of republican freedom can cut its umbilical links to the womb of a national consciousness which had originally given birth to it. Only briefly did the democratic nation-state forge a close link between *ethnos* and *demos*.[4] Citizenship was never conceptually tied to national identity.

The concept of citizenship developed out of Rousseau's notion of self-determination. Initially, 'popular sovereignty' had been under-stood as a delimitation or as the reversal of royal sovereignty and was judged to rest on a contract between a people and its government. Rousseau and Kant, by contrast, did not conceive of popular sovereignty as the transfer of political power from above to below or as its distribution among two contracting parties. Popular sovereignty rather signified the transformation of authoritarian into *self-legislated* power. The social contract is no longer conceived of as a historical pact; it provides an abstract model for the very mode of how political authority is constituted and legitimated. The intention is to purge the remaining strands of *violentia* from the *auctoritas* of the state's powers. In this conception, to take Kant's words, 'legislation can only issue from the concurring and unified will of everyone, to the extent that each decides the same about all and that all decide the same about each. . .'.[5]

This concept of popular sovereignty does not refer to some substantive collective will which would owe its identity to a prior homogeneity of descent or form of life. The consensus achieved in the course of argument in an association of free and equal citizens stems in the final instance from an identically applied *procedure* recognized by all. This procedure for political will formation assumes a differentiated form in the constitution of a democratic state. Thus, in a pluralistic society, the constitution lends expression to a *formal* consensus. The citizens wish to organize their peaceful coexistence in line with principles which meet with the justified agreement of all because they are in the equal interest of all. Such an association is structured by relations of mutual recognition and, given these relations, everyone can expect to be respected by everybody else as free and equal. Everyone should be in a position to expect that all will receive equal protection and respect in his or her violable integrity as a unique individual, as a member of an ethnic or cultural group and as a citizen, that is, as a member of a polity. This idea of a self-determining political community has taken on concrete legal shape in a variety of constitutions, in fact in all political systems of Western Europe and the United States.

Active citizenship

For a long time, however, '*Staatsbürgerschaft*', '*citoyenneté*' or 'citizenship' all only meant, in the language of the law, political membership. It is only recently that the concept has been expanded to cover the status of citizens defined in terms of civil rights.[6] Citizenship as membership of a state only assigns a particular person to a particular nation whose existence is recognized in terms of international law. This definition of membership serves, along with the territorial demarcation of the country's borders, the purpose of a social delimitation of the state. In democratic states, which understand themselves as an association of free and equal citizens, membership depends on the principles of voluntariness. Here, the usual ascriptive characteristics of domicile and birth (*ius soli* and *ius sanguinis*) by no means justify a person being irrevocably subjected to the sovereign authority of that country. They function merely as administrative criteria for attributing to citizens an assumed, implicit concurrence, to which the right to emigrate or to renounce one's citizenship corresponds.[7]

Today, however, the expression '*Staatsbürgerschaft*' or 'citizenship' is not only used to denote membership of a state, but also for a status defined by civil rights. The German Basic Law has no parallel to the Swiss notion of active citizenship (*Aktivbürgerschaft*).[8] However, taking Article 33.1 of the Basic Law as its starting point, mainstream German legal thought has expanded the package of civil rights and duties to generate an overall status of a similar kind.[9] The republican meaning of citizenship is, for example, captured by R. Grawert's work; for him, citizenship has as its reference point the problem of societal self-organization and at its core the political rights of participation and communication. He conceives of citizenship as 'the legal institution via which the individual member of a nation takes part as an active agent in the concrete nexus of state actions'.[10] The status of citizen is constituted above all by those democratic rights which the individual can reflexively lay claim to in order to alter his or her material legal status.

Two mutually contradictory interpretations of such active citizenship capacity vie with each other for pride of place in the philosophy of law. The role of the citizen is given an individualist and instrumentalist reading in the liberal tradition of natural law starting with Locke, whereas a communitarian and ethical understanding of the same has emerged in the tradition of political philosophy that draws on Aristotle. From the first perspective, citizenship is conceived in analogy to the model of received membership in an organization which secures a legal status. From the second, it is conceived in analogy to the model of achieved membership in a self-determining ethical community. In the one interpretation, the individuals remain external to the state, contributing only in a certain manner to its reproduction in return for the benefits of organizational membership. In the other, the citizens are integrated into the political community like parts into a whole; that is, in such a manner that they can only form their personal and social identity in this horizon of shared traditions and intersubjectively recognized institutions. In the former, the citizens are no different from private persons who bring their pre-political interests to bear *vis-à-vis* the state apparatus, whereas in the latter, citizenship can only be realized as a joint practice of self-determination. Charles Taylor has described these two competing concepts of citizenship as follows:

> One [model] focuses mainly on individual rights and equal treatment, as well as on a government performance which takes account of citizen's preferences. This is what has to be secured. Citizen capacity consists mainly in the power to retrieve these rights and ensure equal treatment, as well as to influence the effective decision-makers . . . These institutions have an entirely instrumental significance . . . No value is put on participation in rule for its own sake . . . The other model, by contrast, defines participation in self-rule as of the essence of freedom, as part of what must be secured. This is . . . an essential component of citizen capacity . . . Full participation in self-rule is seen as being able, at least part of the time, to have some part in the forming of a ruling consensus, with which one can identify along with others. To rule and be ruled in turn means that at least some of the time the governors can be 'us' and not always 'them'.[11]

The holist model of a polity in which each citizen is completely bound up is inadequate if one bears in mind many of the aspects of modern politics. Nevertheless, it has an advantage over the organization model, for the latter sets isolated individuals against a state apparatus, the two being linked only via a relation of membership that regulates an exchange of benefits for functionally specified contributions. The holist model emphasizes that political autonomy is a purpose in itself, to be realized not by single persons in the private pursuit of their particular interests but rather only by all together in an intersubjectively shared praxis. In this reading, the citizen's status is constituted by a web of egalitarian relations of mutual recognition. It assumes that everyone can adopt the second person and first person plural perspective of participants – that is, not merely the perspective of an observer or actor orientated towards his or her own success.

Legally guaranteed relations of recognition do not, however, reproduce themselves of their own accord, but rather require the cooperative efforts of the active praxis of citizens, something in which no one can be compelled by legal norms to take part. There are good reasons why modern compulsory law does not apply to the motives and beliefs of its addressees. A legal duty to make active use of democratic rights would have something totalitarian about it; we would feel it to be alien to modern law. As a consequence, the legally constituted status of citizen is dependent on the *accommodatingness* of a consonant background of motives and beliefs of a citizen geared towards the common weal – motives and beliefs that cannot be forced upon him or her legally. In this regard, the republican model of citizenship reminds one that the institutions of constitutional freedom are only worth as much as a population makes of them, and this would be a population *accustomed* to political freedom and well versed in adopting the we-perspective of active self-determination. Therefore, the legally institutionalized role of citizen has to be embedded in the context of a political culture imbued with the concept of freedom. The necessity of such a background seems to justify the communitarians in their insistence that the citizen must identify him- or herself 'patriotically' with his or her particular form of life. Taylor himself emphasizes the requirement of a collective consciousness which arises from identification with the consciously accepted traditions of one's own particular ethical and cultural community: 'The issue is, can our patriotism survive the marginalization of a participatory self-rule? As we have seen, a patriotism is a common identification with a historical community founded on certain values . . . But it must be one whose core values incorporate freedom.'[12]

With this, Taylor appears to contradict our proposition that there is only a historically contingent and not a conceptual connection between republicanism and nationalism. Studied more closely, Taylor's remarks boil down to the statement that the universalist principles of democratic states need an anchoring in the political culture of each country. The principles laid down in the constitution can neither take shape in social practices nor become the driving force for the project of creating an association of free and equal persons, until they are *situated* in the context of the history of a nation of citizens in such a way as to be connected with their motives and convictions.

However, examples of multicultural societies like Switzerland and the United States demonstrate that a political culture in the seedbed of which constitutional principles are rooted by no means has to be based on all citizens sharing the same language or the same ethnic and cultural origins. Rather, the political culture must serve as the common denominator for a constitutional patriotism which simultaneously sharpens an awareness of the multiplicity and integrity of the different forms of life which coexist in a multicultural society. In a future Federal Republic of European States, the same legal principles would also have to be interpreted from the vantage point of different national traditions and histories. One's own national tradition will, in each case, have to be appropriated in such a manner that it is related to and relativized by the vantage points of the other national cultures. It must be connected with the overlapping consensus of a common, supranationally shared political culture of the European Community. Particularist anchoring *of this sort* would in no way impair the universalist meaning of popular sovereignty and human rights.

European citizenship

The political future of the European Community sheds light on the relation between national citizenship and national identity in yet another respect. The concept of national citizenship as developed from Aristotle to Rousseau was, after all, originally tailored to the size of cities and city-states. The transformation of populations into nations which formed states occurred, as we have seen, under the sign of a nationalism which apparently succeeded in reconciling republican ideas with the larger dimensions of modern territorial states. It was, however, in these dimensions covered by the nation-state that modern trade and commerce arose. And, like the bureaucratic state apparatus, the capitalist economy also developed a systemic entelechy of its own. The markets for goods, capital and labour obey their own logic, independent of the intentions of the persons involved. Alongside administrative power, money has thus also become an anonymous medium of societal integration that functions beyond the minds of individual actors. Now, this *system integration* competes with another form of integration running through the consciousness of the actors involved, that is, *social integration* through values, norms and processes of reaching understanding. Just one aspect of social integration is political integration via citizenship. As a consequence, although liberal theories often deny the fact, the relation between capitalism and democracy is fraught with tension.

Examples from Third World countries confirm that there is no linear connection between the emergence of democratic regimes and capitalist modernization. Even the welfare state compromise, practised in the Western democracies since the end of the Second World War, did not come into being automatically. And, finally, the development of the European Community brings, in its own way, this tension between democracy and capitalism to the fore. Here, it is expressed in the vertical divide between the systemic integration of economy and administration at the supranational level – and political integration that thus far works only at the level of the nation-state. The technocratic shape taken by the European Community reinforces doubts whether the normative expectations one associates with the role of the democratic citizen have not actually always been a mere illusion. Did the temporary symbiosis of republicanism and nationalism not only mask the fact that the exacting concept of the citizenship is at best suited for the less-complex relations within an ethnically and culturally homogeneous community?

The 'European Economic Community' has meanwhile become a 'European Community' that proclaims the political will to create a 'European Union'. Leaving India aside, the United States of America provides the only example of such a large edifice of 250 million inhabitants. Having said that, however, the United States is a multicultural society united by the same political culture and (at least at present) the same language, whereas the European Union would be a multilingual state of different nations. This association would still have to exhibit some similarities with de Gaulle's 'Europe of Fatherlands' even if it, and this is to be hoped, were to be more like a Federal Republic than a loose federation of semi-sovereign individual states. The sort of nation-states we have seen to date would continue to exert a strong structural force in such a Europe.

That nation-states constitute a problem along the thorny path to a European Union is, however, less due to their insurmountable claims to sovereignty than to another fact: democratic processes have hitherto only functioned within national borders. So far, the political public sphere is fragmented into national units. The question thus arises whether there can ever be such a thing as European citizenship. And by this I mean not only the possibilities for collective political action across national borders but also the consciousness of 'an obligation toward the European common weal'.[13] As late as 1974, Raymond Aron answered this question with a resolute 'no'. To date, genuine civil rights do not reach beyond national borders.

The administration of justice by the European Court takes the 'Five Freedoms of the Common Market' as its point of orientation and interprets the free exchange of goods, the free movement of labour, the freedom of entrepreneurial domicile, the freedom of service transactions, and the freedom of currency movements as the basic rights. This corresponds with the powers the Treaty of Rome conferred upon the Council of Ministers and the High Commission in Article 3. This, in turn, is to be explained in terms of the goal set out in Article 9: 'The basis of the Community shall be a customs union which extends to include the exchange of all goods.' This goal will have been reached with the advent of the currency union and the establishment of an autonomous central bank. The new level of economic interdependence will give rise to a growing need for coordination in other policy fields as well, such as environmental policy, fiscal and social policy, education policy, etc. And the need for new regulations will again be assessed primarily by criteria of economic rationality, such as securing equal conditions for competition. These tasks will be accomplished by European organizations which have meanwhile meshed to form a dense administrative network. The new elites of bureaucrats are, formally speaking, still accountable to the governments and institutions in their respective country of origin; factually, however, they have grown out of their national context. In this respect, the Brussels authorities can best be equated with the German Central Bank. Professional civil servants form a bureaucracy that is aloof from democratic processes.

For the citizen, this translates into an ever greater gap between being affected by something and participating in changing it. An increasing number of measures decided at a supranational level affect more and more citizens over an ever greater number of areas of life. Given that the role of citizen has hitherto only been institutionalized at the level of the nation-state, citizens have no effective means of debating European decisions and influencing the decision-making processes. M.R. Lepsius' terse statement sums it up: there is no European public opinion.[14] Now, what interests me is the question of whether this disparity is just a passing imbalance that can be set right by the parliamentarization of the Brussels expertocracy or whether these suprastate bureaucracies with their orientation towards sheer economic criteria of rationality merely highlight a general trend that has for long also been gaining momentum within the nation-states. I am thinking of the fact that economic imperatives have gradually become independent of all else and that politics has gradually become a matter of administration, processes that undermine the status of citizen and deny the republican meat of such a status.

Taking England as his example, T.H. Marshall studied the expansion of civil rights and duties in connection with capitalist modernization.[15] His division into *civil, political* and *social* rights is modelled on the well-known legal classification of basic rights. Here, liberal negative rights protect the private legal subject against the state illegally infringing on his or her individual freedom and property; the rights of political participation enable the active citizen to take part in the democratic processes of opinion and will formation; social rights secure the client of the welfare state a minimum of social security. Marshall's analysis supports the thesis that the status of the citizen in modern societies has been expanded and buttressed step by step. The negative rights of individual freedom were first supplemented by democratic rights, and then the two classic types were enhanced by social rights in such a way that ever greater sections of the population gradually acquired full membership.

Even leaving the historical details aside, this suggestion of a more or less linear development only holds for what sociologists term 'inclusion'. In a functionally ever more differentiated society an ever greater number of persons acquire an ever larger number of rights of access to and participation in an ever greater number of subsystems, be these markets, factories and places of work, government offices, courts and standing armies, schools and hospitals, theatres and museums, insurance, public services and goods, political associations and public communications media, political parties, or parliaments. For each individual the number of memberships in organizations therewith multiplies, and the range of options expands. However, this image of linear progress arises from a description that remains neutral towards increases or losses in autonomy; it says nothing about the actual use made of active citizenship by means of which the individual can him- or herself bring influence to bear on democratic changes of his or her own status. It is indeed only political rights of participation which endow the citizen with this kind of self-referential competence. Liberal or negative and social or positive rights can also be conferred by a paternalistic authority. In principle, then, the rule of law and the welfare state can exist without the concomitant existence of democracy. Liberal and social rights remain ambiguous in Western countries where all three categories of rights are institutionalized.

Liberal rights, which have historically crystallized around private ownership, can be grasped from a *functionalist* viewpoint as the institutionalization of a market-steered economy, whereas, from a *normative* viewpoint, they guarantee individual freedoms. Social rights signify from a *functionalist* viewpoint the installation of a welfare bureaucracy, while, from the *normative* viewpoint, they grant the compensatory claims individuals make to a supposedly just distribution of social wealth. It is true that both individual freedom and social security can be considered as the legal basis for the social independence necessary for an effective exercise of political rights in the first place. Yet this link is contingent. For rights of individual freedom and social security can just as well facilitate a privatist retreat from citizenship and a particular 'clientelization' of the citizen's role.

The occurrence of this syndrome, that is, of citizenship reduced to the interests of a client, becomes all the more probable, the more the economy and the state apparatus – which have been institutionalized in terms of the same rights – develop a systemic autonomy and push citizens into the periphery of organizational membership.

As self-regulated systems, economy and administration tend to cut themselves off from their environments and obey only their internal imperatives of money and power. They no longer fit into the model of a self-determining community of citizens. The classic republican idea of the self-conscious political integration of a community of free and equal persons is evidently too concrete and simple a notion to remain applicable to modern conditions, especially if one has in mind a nation, indeed an ethically homogeneous community which is held together by common traditions and a shared history.

The model of a deliberative democracy

Fortunately, modern law is a medium which allows for a much more abstract notion of the citizen's autonomy. Nowadays, the sovereignty of the people has constrained itself to become a procedure of more or less discursive opinion and will formation. Still on a normative level, I assume a networking of different communication flows which, however, should be organized in such a way that they can be supposed to bind the public administration to more or less rational premises and in this way to enforce social and ecological discipline on the economic system without impinging on its intrinsic logic. This provides a model of a deliberative democracy that no longer hinges on the assumption of macro-subjects like the 'people' of 'the' community but on anonymously interlinked discourses or flows of communication. The model shifts the brunt of fulfilling normative expectations from spontaneous sources. Citizenship can today only be enacted in the paradoxical sense of compliance with the procedural rationality of a political will formation, the more or less discursive character of which depends on the vitality of the informal circuit of public communication. An inclusive public sphere cannot be organized as a whole; it depends rather on the stabilizing context of a liberal and egalitarian political culture. At the same time, such a kind of communicative pluralism would still be ineffective unless further conditions could be met. In the first place, deliberations within the decision-making bodies need to be open for and sensitive to the influx of issues, value orientations, contributions and programmes from their informal environments. Only if such an interplay between institutionalized processes of opinion and will formation and those informal networks of public communication occurs can citizenship today mean anything more than an aggregation of pre-political individual interests and the passive enjoyment of rights bestowed upon the individual by the paternalistic authority of the state.

I cannot go into this model in any further detail here.[16] Yet when assessing the chances for a future European citizenship, some empirical hints can at least be gleaned from the historical example of the institutionalization of citizenship within the nation-states. Clearly, the view that sees the rights of citizenship essentially as the product of class struggle is too narrow in focus.[17] Other types of social movement, above all migrations and wars, were the driving force behind the development of a fully fledged status for citizens. In addition, factors that prompted the juridification of new relations of inclusion also had an impact on the political mobilization of a population and thus on the active exercise of given rights of citizenship.[18] These and other related findings allow us to extrapolate with cautious optimism the course European developments could take; thus we are at least not condemned to resign from the outset.

The single market will set in motion even more extensive horizontal mobility and multiply the contacts between members of different nationalities. Immigration from Eastern Europe and the poverty-stricken regions of the Third World will intensify the multicultural diversity of these societies. This will give rise to social tensions. However, if those tensions are processed productively they will enhance political mobilization, in general, and might particularly encourage the new, endogenous type of new social movements – I am thinking of the peace, ecological and women's movements. These tendencies would strengthen the relevance public issues have for the life-world. The increasing pressure of these problems is, furthermore, to be expected, problems for which coordinated solutions are available only at a European level. Given these conditions, communication networks of European-wide public spheres may emerge, networks that may form a favourable context both for new parliamentary bodies of regions that are in the process of merging and for a European Parliament furnished with greater competence.

To date, the member states have not made the legitimation of EC policy the object of controversy. By and large, the national public spheres are culturally isolated from one another. They are anchored in contexts in which political issues only gain relevance against the background of the national histories and national experiences. In the future, however, differentiation could occur in a European culture between a common *political* culture and the branching *national* traditions of art and literature, historiography, philosophy, etc. The cultural elites and the mass media would have an important role to play in this regard. Unlike the American variant, a European constitutional patriotism would have to grow from different interpretations, which the same universalist rights and constitutional principles enjoy by receiving their place in the context of different national histories. Switzerland is an example of how a common politicocultural self-image stands out against the cultural orientations of the different nationalities.

In this context, our task is less to reassure ourselves of our common origins in the European Middle Ages than to develop a new political self-confidence commensurate with the role of Europe in the world of the twenty-first century. Hitherto, world history has accorded the empires that have come and gone but *one* appearance on the stage. This is not only true of the rising and falling empires in the Old World, but also for modern states like Portugal, Spain, England, France and Russia. It now appears as if Europe as a whole is being given a second chance. It will not be able to make use of this in terms of the power politics of yester-year, but only under changed premises, namely a non-imperial process of reaching understanding with and learning from other cultures.

Notes

1 Peter Glotz, *Der Irrweg des Nationalstaats* (Stuttgart, 1990).

2 M.R. Lepsius, 'Der europäische Nationalstaat', in M.R. Lepsius (ed.), *Interessen, Ideen und Institutionen* (Opladen, 1990), p. 256ff.

3 See the article on 'Nation' in *Historisches Wörterbuch der Philosophie*, 6, pp. 406–14.

4 M.R. Lepsius, 'Ethnos und Demos', in *Interessen*, pp. 247–55.

5 I. Kant, *Metaphysik der Sitten, Rechtslehre*, p. 46.

6 See on what follows R. Grawert, 'Staatsangehörigkeit und Staatsbürgerschaft', *Der Staat*, 23 (1984), pp. 179–204.

7 P.H. Schuck and R.M. Smith, *Citizenship without Consent* (New Haven, 1985), ch. 1. Admittedly, not everywhere is the normative meaning of national citizenship consistently uncoupled from ascriptive characteristics. Article 116 of the German Basic Law, for example, introduces a notion of so-called 'German by status', someone who belongs to the German people according to an objectively confirmed 'attestation of membership in the cultural community', without at the same time being a German citizen. Such a person enjoys the privilege of being able to become a German citizen, although this is now contested by some constitutional experts.

8 R. Winzeler, *Die politischen Recht des Aktivbürgers nach Schweizerischem Bundesrecht* (Berne, 1983).

9 K. Hesse, *Grundzüge des Verfassungsrechts* (Heidelberg, 1990), p. 113, states: 'In their function as subjective rights, the basic rights determine and secure the foundations of the individual's legal status. In their function as objective basic components of a democratic and constitutional social order, they insert the individual in this order, which can itself only become a reality if these rights are given real shape. The status of the individual in terms of constitutional law, as grounded in and guaranteed by the basic rights laid out in the Basic Law, is thus a material legal status, i.e. a status with concretely determined contents, a status which neither the

individual nor the state's powers can unrestrictedly adopt at will. This status in constitutional law forms the core of the general status of national citizenship, which, along with the basic rights . . . is laid down in law.'

10 R. Grawert, 'Staatsvolk und Staatsangehörigkeit', in J. Isensee and P. Kirchhof (eds), *Handbuch des Staatsrechts* (Heidelberg, 1987), p. 684ff.

11 C. Taylor, 'The liberal–communitarian debate', in N. Rosenblum (ed.), *Liberalism and the Moral Life* (Cambridge, MA., 1989), p. 178f.

12 Ibid., p. 178.

13 P. Kielmannsegg, 'Ohne historisches Vorbild', *Frankfurter Allgemeine Zeitung*, 7 December 1990.

14 M.R. Lepsius, 'Die Europäische Gemeinschaft'. Paper presented to the 20th Congress of German Sociologists, Frankfurt am Main, 1990.

15 T.H. Marshall, *Citizenship and Social Class* (Cambridge University Press, Cambridge, 1950).

16 See J. Habermas, 'Volkssouveränität ais Verfahren', in J. Habermas (ed.), *Die Moderne – ein unvollendetes Projekt* (Leipzig, 1990), p. 180ff.

17 B.S. Turner, *Citizenship and Capitalism: The Debate over Reformism* (Allen & Unwin, London, 1986).

18 J.M. Barbalet, *Citizenship* (Open University Press, Milton Keynes, 1988).

4

FOUR CONCEPTIONS OF CITIZENSHIP

Herman van Gunsteren

The republic

A citizen is both governor and governed. In a republic, the force of arms and all other powers of public authorities, such as political decision-making, government and the administration of justice, are exercised by citizens and their fellow-citizens. Even a political community formally headed by a monarch, as in the case of The Netherlands, where citizens nevertheless determine the course of events, is called a republic.

Although it is nowadays very common, a republic remains a particular and awe-inspiring phenomenon. Citizens within a republic perform functions that were traditionally attributed to others or to outsiders. Armed force and legislation inevitably play a crucial role in the founding of a political community, as well as in the accounts and rituals that are later spun around the irretraceable founding act. Within the bounds of armed force and legislation, peace and freedom can be found by ordinary people. Armed force and legislation constitute dangerous 'supertasks', the fulfilment of which is controlled and protected by special guarantees. The state claims monopoly over these tasks. In a republic, these tasks are not performed by outsiders, but by those who are otherwise equally subject to public authority. This double role is unusual and awe-inspiring. It is all the more remarkable when one considers that in a republic the exercise of authority is geared towards recognition and regulation of differences between the citizen and the state, and not towards elimination of those differences.

In order to practise this double role of governor and subject, citizens must display a minimum of autonomy, sound judgement and loyalty. In the past it was evident that, given these require-ments, citizenship was not granted to everyone. Those who are enslaved or addicted, who formally or materially in their way of life or for subsistence are dependent on the arbitrary will of others, cannot be citizens. The same goes for those incapable of reasonable observation and judgement. Loyalty can only be expected of persons who make a tangible contribution to the common business and are therefore directly concerned with careful public decision-making and implementation of decisions. The supreme index that traditionally proved fulfilment of the three requirements was the possession of property, in particular landed property.

Citizenship for all

Modern republics strive for citizenship for all people, including those who are not wealthy. They provide welfare facilities that protect the less wealthy from having to give up their independent political judgement and action for the maintenance of their lives, sustenance and other elementary necessities. Social security and welfare assistance are thus the functional equivalents of property as a prerequisite for citizenship. The same goes for arrangements that aim to provide those not belonging to the elite group of property owners with access to the knowledge, culture and organization that are necessary for the effective practice of citizenship in modern society.

Conditions for citizenship have always existed. Traditionally, maintenance of and control over admission to citizenship was a role played by the state. Novel to this century, however, is not that the state maintains the conditions for citizenship, but that it assists individuals aspiring to citizenship to surmount the obstacles to admission – by helping them to obtain the qualities required for admission, but also by removing the obstacles and lowering the demands. This is where the state enters into conflict with its task of maintaining the requirements for admission. Flippant treatment of these requirements endangers the quality of citizenship. Until recently, this was not perceived as a problem. Attention was focused on practices of liberation (admission to citizenship) and not on practices of freedom (competent, sensible and responsible use of freedom). Citizenship was all right; the trick was to get more people involved in it.

Lately this has changed. Not only has admission to citizenship become an important and problematic issue; so has citizenship itself. How has this change come about? First, citizenship has become a coveted and scarce good in the international movement of people. Secondly, an increasing number of citizens have started to use (misuse) the system of provisions and entitlements (playing the system) in a way that is contrary to the civil spirit and competence traditionally expected of them. They outmanoeuvre the system. (It is possible that we are not dealing here with increased 'misuse' as such, but that in the modern context of subtle steering of the system, this 'misuse' may have a more disturbing impact than before.) Thirdly, the public institutional setting is shifting. The sovereign nation-state has gradually been replaced by a multitude of centres of authority and of loyalty, thereby creating the possibility of multiple citizenship (e.g. European in addition to national citizenship). Fourthly, endeavours by the state to remove the obstacles hampering admission to citizenship have come in for a great deal of criticism. Welfare state provisions are not considered as liberating but rather as keeping people tied in their poverty and their dependency. Help from the state is in fact an obstacle to citizenship. Thus the question is no longer how large the obstacles should be and how people can be carried over them as quickly as possible, but also whether the state should offer this help at all.

In short, citizenship has become in many respects a problematic issue. Problems occur in the practices of admission (asylum, European citizenship, education) and membership requirements (social security, employment, the 'underclass'), but also in questions of competence (civic-mindedness, civil servants as citizens, conflicts within democratic institutions) and pluralism (minorities and the law, senior citizens, businesses as quasi-citizens). These developments naturally entail a revision of the established theories and conceptions of citizenship. In the following, I shall discuss three conceptions of citizenship and later examine how they fail in today's society. I will then sketch a notion of neo-republican citizenship which forms a synthesis of the other three conceptions and grafts more successfully onto the present recondite 'civil society'.

The citizen as calculating bearer of rights and preferences

This is the liberal-individualistic conception of citizenship. The utilitarian version assumes that all individuals maximize their own benefit. They calculate what choice of action will result in the highest product of value attributed to the desired situation multiplied by the probability that this situation will occur ($C = V \times P$, i.e. Choice is Value times Probability). The individual rights version allows individuals to base their calculations on their own rights limited by their respect for the rights of others. The rights themselves may or may not be derived from utilitarian considerations. It is important to note that both versions take the individual with his or her rights, opinions and choices for granted, and that both explain and vindicate politics in terms of non-political individual entities. Citizenship and other political institutions are expedients that are only accepted conditionally, that is as long as they form conditions in the individual's calculation for maximal benefit.

There are two main problems with this conception of citizenship. First, how can individuals be prevented from destroying each other on the basis of their reciprocal benefit? The war of all against all, the 'tragedy of the commons', the unemployed who receive unemployment benefit yet illegally work – these are all cases illustrating the same problem. The problem is individualism; it is not that people are 'evil'. Friendliness too can cause people to destroy each other. Think of a burning concert hall with a single exit where everybody says 'after you'. Inverted congestion. Secondly, what forms the individual? Insights and preferences of the autonomous individual may well originate from an impure source. Information may be biased or senseless; preference may arise in a fit of anger. Must they be accepted as unassailable, even if it is clear that the bearer of these preferences would have rejected them had he or she known how they had originated? Is it not an internally inconsistent ideal to see an individual as fully autonomous, and his or her preferences and insights as entirely disconnected from coincidental outside circumstances? Such an individual disconnected from all coincidence is nothing – cannot, in fact, have any preferences (except by coincidence, but precisely there lies his or her independence). Yet is the ideal of an individual entirely determined by coincidental circumstances not similarly inconsistent? Such a person is not an individual, but a cue ball.

These problems were never urgent as long as people showed 'responsible' behaviour. They attended elections and did not vote for anti-democratic parties. They had health insurance and did not declare themselves sick unless they really were. Those days are over. Many people no longer set foot in the voting booth; anti-democratic parties obtain votes; people work without paying taxes, pretend illness and nevertheless continue earning money elsewhere, and skilfully dodge efforts to distinguish cheaters from 'rightful' claimants. To this purpose they may well use the guarantees protecting individual privacy.

None of the suggested answers to these problems has been effective, that is, not as long as they have been conceived within the framework of individualistic citizenship. It is said that the quality of civil democracy depends upon such matters as civic-mindedness, religion, education in democratic rules or the development of a public ethic. A total absence of these things means that democracy cannot exist. To embrace them too intensely, however, would mean the same. In the former case, democracy would perish from self-seeking, in the latter from fanaticism. The challenge is to find the happy medium. Even if these views bear some truth in them, they do not offer a solution to the problems of individualistic citizenship.

Appeals for responsibility and civic-mindedness serve little purpose. Civic-mindedness will not arise, nor develop, by being called for. Civic-mindedness, legitimacy and public support arise as a by-product generated by other activities and events. They do not come into existence by directing our will, intention or manipulation towards them. The desire is contrary to the nature of the desired result, just as is the case with the will to fall asleep or the yearning to be spontaneous.

De Tocqueville showed how, in the American democracy, religion maintained individuals within reasonable limits of freedom.[1] Yet a non-believer cannot be converted to belief on the grounds that this is conducive to peace between individuals. Dahl claimed that consensus on basic norms is necessary in order to make a democracy or a polyarchy work.[2] Education directed towards inculcating such consensus as a matter of course may be an education *leading to* freedom; it is not, however, an education *in* freedom. The development of a relatively independent public ethic continues to stagnate as long as we try to deduce it from a variety of private ethics.[3]

These efforts to circumvent the weaknesses of the individualistic premise call upon actual historical circumstances, upon independent elements in the public domain, or upon *rational* calculation. Thus however, they conflict with the individual non-political and non-historical premise, whose weaknesses they are expected to repair. Those who invoke actual historical circumstances arrive at a communitarian concept of citizenship; those who appeal to independent elements in the public domain arrive at a republican concept of citizenship. These will presently be discussed in more depth. Those who appeal to rational calculation, for example rational motives for belonging to a religion, could be asked the following question: can one, even if one has a deep desire to do so, become religious or become a member of a community sharing the same destiny on the sole basis of rational calculation? We can also ask 'Why be rational?'. This question is all the more cogent now that postmodern conviction, which is increasingly supported, also exposed rationality as contingent and variable. The counter-question is now 'Why should I adhere to your notion of rationality?'

The citizen as a member of a community

This conception strongly emphasizes that being a citizen means belonging to a historically developed community. Individuality is derived from it and determined in terms of it. In this vision, judicious action operates within the limits of what is accepted by the community. Loyalty and education in loyalty cause both the community and the individuals belonging to it to flourish.

There is much to be said in favour of this conception. First, it avoids the problems of individualistic citizenship pointed out above. Individuals are formed by the community. If they conform to the codes of behaviour that have been taught to them, they will ensure the continued existence of the community and of each other. They simply repeat the successful formula that enabled the community to grow and survive. Deviation from the code is considered to be corruption and must be resisted. A community that is declining can be saved by fighting corruption and returning to its origins, its beginnings. Thus authority and the successful formula may be restored.

A second reason for advocating the communitarian conception of citizenship lies in the insight that identity and stability of character cannot be realized without the support of a community of friends and like-minded kindred. A person with a strong character is steadfast in changing circumstances and is not easily knocked off balance. For most people, however, such constancy depends upon the continued existence and membership of a community of roughly like-minded and similarly acting mates, of shared life-styles. Research and historical experience prove time and again that the parties involved, including ourselves, systematically underestimate this dependence.[4] Individual autonomy and competent judgement are not what they appear to be. They are dependent upon the community against which they often brace themselves. This dependence remains hidden in a naive self-consciousness. Individualists who have lost their naivety and recognize this dependence will wish to pay more respect to the community, in order to maintain (their) individuality. This is often impossible, however, since the community is for them an expedient. This is contrary to what is claimed to be the essence of a community, namely its existence as a natural and valuable context of action and judgement. A community that is merely expedient is not a community.

We are already discussing the objections to the communitarian conception of citizenship. The first objection is that awareness of the usefulness or the necessity of a community does not provide a sufficiently strong basis for the maintenance of such a community, nor for belonging to it. In modern societies, communities cannot be taken for granted. There is a plurality of communities and of individual combinations of memberships. In such a society, conscious creation and cultivation of a community that can be taken for granted is an internal contradiction.

A second objection to the communitarian perspective is less concerned with how realistic it is than how desirable it is. Communities place notorious restrictions on freedom. Emancipation has often meant deliverance from the compelling and unjust bondage of community. The emphasis on 'right thinking', which easily emerges in communities that cultivate their own existence, is frightening. The modern state offers protection against such dangers. It limits and regulates the grasp of communities and protects individuals against it. Considering this aspect, efforts by the government to strengthen the communitarian perspective are all the more suspect.

The view that individuality, autonomy and judgement cannot exist without a common basis does not necessarily entail acceptance of the communitarian perspective. A community is both indispensable and dangerous. The state must not be identified with the communities it 'manages'. The state allows room for the existence and the creation of communities, and tempers their excesses. Yet what is it that enables the state to do so? What given community offers the context for this? It is the *public* community, the republic.

Republican citizenship

The republican perspective may be seen as a particular variant of the communitarian idea. A single community, namely the public community, is given the main role. Courage, devotion, military discipline and statecraft are the republican virtues. Serving the public community may make individuality appear and enable the individual to mark his or her place in history. This is where he or she achieves fulfilment and possibly happiness ('public happiness').[5]

The drawbacks of this classical republican conception of citizenship are obvious. Military virtue is dangerous in politics and must be kept within bounds. This conception pays insufficient attention to economics and trade, as well as to the milder facets and fulfilments of private life. Republican virtues are uniformly masculine. The republican perspective makes one community absolute and shows little appreciation for the particular meaning and diversity of other communities.

Ancient theories in present-day society

The three conceptions of citizenship considered above are unsatisfactory. They offer too little guidance. This is because the preconditions they require are no longer fulfilled and cannot be realized by applying the theories. Social relationships and processes largely take form outside the social framework presupposed by the older theories. The theories are no longer suitable for present-day society.

Modern society is not a 'civil society' of autonomous individuals. Large organizations and accumulations of capital are the main determinants of affairs. Individuals, even those at the top, are no heroes, but well-disciplined managers and people made adult through therapy, guided by a keenly perceived intertwining of personal gain and the benefit of the organization for which they work. Instead of friendships they have networks of relationships.

In this corporate society, we find a stunning variety of 'communities', some of which remain in existence for a longer, some for a shorter period of time. Besides the familiar communities of nationality, religion, trade unions and corporate life, we now find a host of less familiar and less established bonds that often play an important role in the lives of individuals, but that we cannot easily call communities. Government bodies, too, have lost their traditional place in modern society. The nation-state has become but one locus of authority amidst a field containing many others. The proliferation of communities and governing bodies in corporate society brings consequences with it.

A first consequence is that political and social identities have become less stable and more varied. The individual – the substrate of the citizen – is a bouquet. He/she composes his/her own mixed identity out of various connections and bonds. This individual is not the natural bearer of civic-mindedness and civic virtue, nor is he/she naturally inclined (however often this may be claimed) to calculate all action in terms of his/her own wealth and power. The preferences, perceptions and ways of 'calculating' of the modern individual may vary. He/she no longer derives them from the established bonds of work, home and the state. The articulation and aggregation of desires and requirements of citizens – middle-class society – that fit these traditional bonds often do little justice to the individuality, the self-composed bouquet, of the present-day citizen.

A second implication of the proliferation of bodies of government and communities in corporate society is the disappearance of a relatively homogeneous middle class that used to form the backbone of the stable republic of citizens. This class was composed of those not rich enough to buy the support of others, and not poor enough to sell their vote, and who had a vested interest in the continued existence of the republic. Until recently, this class was made up of small independent businesses as well as paid employees and households that lived on their incomes. The rise of individualism has dissolved the unity of households. Postmodern life-styles and post-industrial processes of production have caused the old middle class to dwindle to a minority that has rapidly lost its attraction for new recruits.

A third consequence of the developments described above concerns the direction of government. Planning of civil society is, today even less possible than it was in the past. From the point of view of those steering it, society is less and less knowable. The categories in which government seeks to represent reality (using numbers and diagrams) no longer fit the processes that they are expected to describe. There seems to be widespread awareness that we need new categories and coordinates. Yet when we have to specify what those categories should be, we are clueless and often talk at cross-purposes without reaching a new consensus. We struggle on with the old categories and coordinates and find our bearings as best we can, without conviction or commitment, with all kinds of *ad hoc* retouched images. Planning is certainly out of the question now. Good steering is characterized by 'thriving on chaos'.[6] We call this society that is insufficiently knowable from the point of view of its leaders TUS: The Unknown Society.

In present-day society, matters are not determined by established communities, nor by predictably calculating individuals, nor by militarily virtuous servants to the public cause. These do exist, but play a variable role in a changing tide of other actors. None of the three conceptions of citizenship discussed above can be realized in present-day society. Shall we then dismiss citizenship as an unattainable ideal? No, this conclusion would be premature. It is true that none of the three conceptions can be simply realized, but elements can be used to build a conception of citizenship that is meaningful for the present day. Call it fabrication, synthesis or 'bricolage' – we are working with given pieces: grown institutions developed over the years, patterns of thought and ways of acting. We baptize the product 'neo-republican citizenship'.

Neo-republican citizenship

The neo-republican conception of citizenship includes elements from the communitarian, the republican and the individualistic trains of thought.

First of all, a few communitarian elements. The citizen is a member of a *public* community, the republic. For the citizen as such, this community occupies a central position. Yet from the point of view of the individual (the person who, among other things, is a citizen) this community is but one among many others, albeit a community with a special position, just as the Dutch Central Bank is a bank among others, with a special position and task. It is charged with guarding the structure that enables other banks to carry out their activities properly. Similarly, it is the task of the public community to guard the structure that makes it possible for other communities to develop their activities. The task of the republic is to organize plurality. What is special about a civic political community is that while its interference with other communities in a society is temporarily and practically direct, it is always, in the last resort, indirect. Interference is effectuated by the citizens. The republic creates and protects the freedom of individuals to form communities, to join or to reject them.

The neo-republican conception of citizenship also bears republican traits. Virtue is not alien to the civic republic, but it is not the military virtue of the olden days. Rather, it concerns debating, reasonableness, democracy, choice, plurality and carefully limited use of violence. The term virtue implies that more is needed than simply abiding by the rules. It is a matter of sensible, competent and responsible treatment of authority, situations and positions of power. This cannot be exhaustively laid down in rules. Such competence is essential for the effectuation of citizenship. A chairperson presiding over a meeting, who does not break the rules but is otherwise incompetent, is a nuisance, as we may all have experienced.

The emphasis on competence must, of course, not be exaggerated, although it may be temporarily necessary to grant undivided attention to this neglected dimension of public intercourse. Virtue means not only competence, but also ethics in the sense of decent behaviour. The civic republic has autonomous ethics of the public domain that are not purely derived from private ethics or opinions, but are rooted in the public domain itself. Because individuals in their functions as citizens are of central importance in the public domain, such private ethics and opinions do play a role, but never more than a mediating, indirect one. A citizen's contribution is more than the mere sum of the opinions and desires he or she has as a (non-civic) individual.

What is the position of the individual in the neo-republican conception of citizenship? Citizenship is an office in the public community. This means that a citizen is not identical to the ordinary person, or the entire person. It also means that qualifications are required for admission to and the exercise of citizenship. The republic must not only facilitate these, but must also formulate and maintain the required qualifications. In the republic, citizenship is the primary office. The so-called office holders are primarily citizens who, as a part of their exercise of citizenship, perform a special duty. They may at times do or not do things that 'normal' citizens are not entitled to. Yet the existence of these special powers must not support the misunderstanding that such officials cease to be citizens as soon as they accept and fulfil their office. Precisely because these offices are so susceptible, we want them to be held and their execution to be checked by fellow-citizens. Following the Second World War, holders of public office were called upon to legitimize their actions during the occupation on the grounds of their responsibility as citizens for their fellow-citizens.

The government does not wait for individuals to present themselves spontaneously as citizens, it also fosters the formation of people into independent and competent citizens. Individuals are not naturally given, but socially formed. The republic does not simply leave the 'reproduction' of citizens to existing communities, but verifies whether the social formation enjoined by those communities allows for admission to citizenship. Where this is not the case, or where people lack the formative support of the community, the government interferes. The task of reproducing citizens is implied in every government action. Every government action can and may be examined in terms of its effect on (the reproduction of) citizenship, just as we now judge nearly all government action in terms of its effect on the financial deficit.

The assimilation of elements stemming from the earlier concepts brings the neo-republican conception of citizenship into focus. It is characterized by the following core elements.

1 The neo-republican citizen is autonomous, loyal, capable of sound judgement and fulfils the double role of governor and governed. He/she differs from former citizens because his/her autonomy is guaranteed by the republic, because his/her sound judgement emerges mainly in competent treatment of plurality

and because his/her loyalty is directed towards the public organization of plurality itself, the republic.

2   The *organization of pluralism* is the task of the republic. Whenever it is necessary for the execution of this task, normativity must be overtly displayed and must not be avoided or hustled away. This means, among other things, that when the functioning of the republic demands certain norms, these must be enforced in the public domain, and not that the government moulds the private sphere in such a way that it starts generating the norms 'spontaneously'.

3   For the '*reproduction of citizens*', that is the formation of people into autonomous individuals, capable of sound judgement and members of a public community sharing a common fate, the government must assume the leading role. In today's setting, citizenship does not spring up ready-made from society. It is a public responsibility to combine elements in plural society in such a way that their mutual interaction in the public domain results in citizenship. Citizenship is learned and confirmed primarily by its exercising, and in the organization of plurality. Family, church, school and other connections are important and possibly indispensable contributions, but in a plural society they can never be the officially designated sites where citizenship is defined and the citizen is formed.

4   Citizenship stands for a *political position of equality*. Citizenship modifies (both influences and changes) other, not strictly political, relations by demanding that they do not render admission to citizenship practically illusory. Citizenship does not require social equality. The opposite of citizenship is not inequality, but slavery (old and new combinations of powerlessness, humiliation and long-term imprisonment in relationships). In the perspective of citizenship, inequalities are acceptable as long as they do not smack of servility and do not hamper equal admission to citizenship.

5   Citizenship is an *office* in the republic. This somewhat uncommon designation indicates (*a*) that the citizen is not identical to the entire or the ordinary person; (*b*) that the admission to and the exercise of citizenship are linked to requirements of competence; and (*c*) that citizenship is an office among others in the republic, an office that, depending on circumstances, can modify the fulfilment of other offices.

6   It follows that the question of reproduction of citizenship can arise in all areas. Especially in the public domain, every action can be seen in terms of what it implies for citizenship. Citizenship provides a normative and informative viewpoint which,

in conflicts of loyalty, attributes responsibility where it is due, namely to the independently judging citizen who is capable of both governing and being governed.

Variants of such a neo-republican conception of citizenship, though not identically termed, are to be found in the works of Dahrendorf, Oldfield and Barber. There are differences, both in theory and in the practices which the authors choose to highlight. Citizenship always has its local and historical elements. Yet in spite of all these differences, there is an unmistakable common train of thought: the public community as a special community among others, individual citizenship as a product of the activities of citizens within the republic.

Notes

The English translation is by A.F.D. Paret.

1 A. de Tocqueville, *De la Democratie en Amerique* (various editions).

2 R. Dahl, *Democracy and its Critics* (Yale University Press, New Haven, 1989).

3 H.R. van Gunsteren, 'The ethical context of bureaucracy and performance analysis', in F. Kaufmann (ed.), *The Public Sector – Challenge for Coordination and Learning* (De Gruyter, Berlin, 1991).

4 M. Nussbaum, *The Fragility of Goodness* (Cambridge University Press, London, 1986); M. Douglas, *How Institutions Think* (Syracuse University Press, Syracuse, NY, 1986); M. Sandel, *Liberalism and the Limits of Justice* (Cambridge University Press, Cambridge, 1982); S. Milgram, *Obedience to Authority*, Tavistock, London, 1974).

5 See, for the use of this term, H. Arendt, *On Revolution* (The Viking Press, New York, 1965), esp. p. 124.

6 T. Peters, *Thriving on Chaos* (Macmillan, London, 1988).

5

CITIZENSHIP AND THE INNER-CITY GHETTO POOR

William Julius Wilson

Poverty, like other aspects of class inequality, is a consequence not only of differential distribution of economic and political privileges and resources, but of differential access to culture as well. In an industrial society groups are stratified in terms of the material assets or resources they control, the benefits and privileges they receive from these resources, the cultural experiences they have accumulated from historical and existing economic and political arrangements, and the influence they yield because of those arrangements. Accordingly, group variation in life-styles, norms and values is related to the variations in access to organizational channels of privilege and influence.[1]

If we follow T.H. Marshall's classic thesis on the development of citizenship, we see that the more this fundamental principle (the organic link tying poverty to the social class and racial structure of society) is recognized or acknowledged in Western society, the more the emphasis on the rights of citizens will tend to go beyond civil and political rights to include social rights, that is 'the whole range from the right to a modicum of economic welfare and security to the right to share to the full in the social heritage and to live the life of a civilized being according to the standards prevailing in the society'.[2]

However, as critics of American approaches to the study of poverty and welfare have shown repeatedly, concerns about the civil and political aspects of citizenship in the United States have overshadowed concerns about the social aspects of citizenship (that is, the 'social' rights to employment, economic security, education and health) because of a strong belief system that denies the social origins and social significance of poverty and welfare.

After analysing findings from national survey data collected in 1969 and then again in 1980, Kluegel and Smith concluded that 'Most Americans believe that opportunity for economic advancement

ment is widely available, that economic outcomes are determined by individuals' efforts and talents (or their lack) and that in general economic inequality is fair'.[3] Indeed, the national surveys revealed that, when given items representing an individualistic explanation for poverty (for example, lack of effort or ability, poor morals, poor work skills), and a structural explanation (for example, lack of adequate schooling, low wages, lack of jobs), Americans over-whelmingly favoured the individualistic causes over the structural ones. The most popular items, in decreasing order of importance, were 'lack of thrift or proper money management skills', 'lack of effort', 'lack of ability or talent', 'attitudes from one's family background that impede social mobility', 'failure of society to provide good schools', and 'loose morals and drunkenness'. Except for the 'failure of society to provide good schools', all of these items represent individualistic understandings of the causes of poverty. Structural factors such as 'low wages', 'failure of industry to provide jobs', and 'racial discrimination' were considered least important of all. The ordering of these factors remained virtually unchanged over the period 1969–1980.[4] Similar results from other surveys indicate that this stability of opinion is not an artefact of wording.[5]

In 1978 the French social scientist Robert Castel argued that the paradox of poverty in affluent American society has rested on the notion that 'the poor are individuals who themselves bear the chief responsibility for their condition. As a result the politics of welfare centers around the management of individual deficiencies'.[6] From the building of almshouses in the late nineteenth century to President Johnson's 'War on Poverty', Americans have failed to emphasize the social rights of the poor, 'rights whose interpretation is independent of the views of the agencies charged with dispensing assistance'.[7]

The data from public opinion polls support this argument. They indicate that Americans tend to be far more concerned about the duties or social obligations of the poor, particularly the welfare poor, than about their social rights as American citizens.[8] As far back as the New Deal, Americans have persistently debated whether recipients of welfare cheques should be required to work. Public opinion polls over the years have revealed strong support for a work requirement for those on welfare. For example, a Harris poll taken in 1972 showed that 89 per cent of the respondents were 'in favour of making people on welfare go to work'. A 1977 NBC poll revealed that 93 per cent of respondents felt that able-bodied welfare recipients should be required to work at public jobs.[9] Survey data also suggest that public sentiment against welfare has tended to increase over the past few years. The percentage of respondents in a national poll who agreed with the anti-welfare statement that we are 'spending too much money on welfare programs in this country' increased from 61 per cent in 1969 to 81 per cent in 1980; those who agreed with the anti-welfare statement that 'most people getting welfare are not honest about their needs' rose from 71 per cent in 1969 to 77 per cent in 1980; finally, those who concurred with the pro-welfare view that 'most people on welfare who can work try to find jobs so they can support themselves' declined from 47 per cent in 1969 to 31 per cent in 1980.[10]

A further survey suggests that underlying such overwhelming public sentiment against welfare is the belief that it is the moral fabric of individuals, not inequities in the social and economic structure of society, that is the cause of the problem. Indeed, this survey uncovered widespread sentiment for the notion that most welfare recipients do not share the majority view about the importance of hard work. A majority of the whites polled in this study disagreed with the pro-welfare statement that 'most welfare recipients do need help and could not get along without welfare'. There was strong sentiment for the view that welfare reform, in the words of one respondent, should be 'to get people motivated and become part of the system'. Finally, this study emphasized 'that there is today, as there has been for years, general agreement – shared by whites and non-whites alike – that many people on welfare could be working, that many people on welfare cheat, and that a lot of money spent on behalf of the poor has been wasted.'[11]

However, it should be pointed out that, although the term 'welfare' evokes strong negative reactions in the surveys, the term 'needy' does not. Questions on helping the needy tend to elicit favourable responses. In the dominant American belief system on poverty and welfare a distinction is made between the 'deserving poor' and the 'undeserving poor'. The deserving poor include groups such as the aged and the disabled – groups which are seen as needy and whose poverty, as Joel Handler puts it, is seen as being 'caused by "accidents", factors beyond the individual's control and for which there is no blame. The deserving poor are presumed to be law-abiding members of society rather than malingerers, cheats, and deviants'.[12]

The heavy emphasis on the individual traits of the poor and on the duties or social obligations of welfare recipients is not unique to the general public. This 'common wisdom' has been uncritically integrated in the work of many poverty researchers. Throughout the 1960s and 1970s, the expanding network of poverty researchers in the United States, with the notable exception of the liberal urban field researchers, paid considerable attention to the question of individuals' work attitudes and the association between income maintenance programmes and the work ethic of the poor. They consistently ignored the effects of basic economic transformations and cyclical processes on the work experiences and prospects of the poor. In an examination of American approaches to the study of poverty from a European perspective, Walter Korpi has pointed out that 'efforts to explain poverty and inequality in the United States . . . appear primarily to have been sought in terms of the characteristics of the poor'.[13] Whereas poverty researchers in the United States have conducted numerous studies on the work motivation of the poor, problems of human capital (whereby poverty is discussed as, if not reduced to, a problem of lack of education and occupational skills) and the effects of income-maintenance programmes on the supply of labour, they have largely neglected to study the impact of extremely high levels of postwar unemployment on impoverished Americans. Ironically, 'In Europe, where unemployment has been considerably lower, the concerns of politicians as well as researchers have been keyed much more strongly to the question of unemployment', states Korpi. 'It is an intellectual paradox that living in a *society that has been a sea of unemployment*, American poverty researchers have concentrated their research interests on the work motivation of the poor'.[14]

Another irony is that, despite this narrow focus, these very American researchers have consistently uncovered empirical findings that undermine, not support, assumptions about the negative effects of welfare receipt on individual initiative and motivation. Yet these assumptions persist among policy-makers and 'the paradox of continuing high poverty during a period of general prosperity has contributed to the recently emerging consensus that welfare must be reformed'.[15] Although it is reasonable to argue that policy-makers are not aware of a good deal of the empirical research on the effects of welfare, the General Accounting Office (GAO), an investigative arm of Congress, released a study in early 1987 which reported that there was no conclusive evidence for the prevailing belief that welfare discourages individuals from working, breaks up two-parent families or affects the child-bearing rates of unmarried women, even young unmarried women.

The GAO report reached these conclusions after reviewing the results of more than a hundred empirical studies on the effects of welfare completed since 1975, analysing the case files of more than 1,200 families receiving public assistance in four states, and interviewing officials from federal, state and local government agencies. Although these conclusions should come as no surprise to poverty researchers familiar with the empirical literature, they should have generated a stir among congressmen, many of whom have no doubt been influenced by the highly publicized works of conservative scholars such as George Gilder, Charles Murray and Lawrence Mead that ascribe, without direct empirical evidence, persistent poverty and other social dislocations to the negative effects of welfare and the development of a welfare culture. But, apparently, rigorous scientific argument is no match for the dominant belief system: the views of congressmen were apparently not significantly altered by the GAO report.

The growth of social dislocations among the inner-city poor and the continued high rates of poverty have led an increasing number of policy-makers to conclude that something should be done about the current welfare system to halt what they perceive to be the breakdown of the norms of citizenship. Indeed, a liberal–conservative consensus on welfare reform has recently emerged which features two themes: (*a*) the receipt of welfare should be predicated on reciprocal responsibilities whereby society is obligated to provide assistance to welfare applicants who, in turn, are obligated to behave in socially approved ways; and (*b*) able-bodied adult welfare recipients should be required to prepare themselves for work, to search for employment and to accept jobs when they are offered. These points of agreement were reflected in the discussions of the welfare reform legislation recently passed in the United States Congress.

These two themes are based on the implicit assumption that a sort of mysterious 'welfare ethos' exists that encourages public assistance recipients to avoid their obligations as citizens to be educated, to work, to support their families and to obey the law. In other words, and in keeping with the dominant American belief system, *it is the moral fabric of individuals, not the social and economic structure of society, that is taken to be the root of the problem.* I believe that this belief system has implications for the way the problems of truly disadvantaged citizens are addressed in American society.

The underclass in American society

In the United States historical discrimination and a migration to large metropolises that kept the urban minority population relatively young created a problem of weak labour force attachment among urban blacks and, especially since 1970, made them particularly vulnerable to the industrial and geographical changes in the economy. The shift from goods-producing to service-producing industries, the increasing polarization of the labour market into low-wage and high-wage sectors, innovations in technology, the relocation of manufacturing industries out of central cities, and periodic recessions have forced up the rate of black joblessness (unemployment and non-participation in the labour market), despite the passage of anti-discrimination legislation and the creation of affirmative action programmes. The rise in joblessness has in turn helped trigger an increase in the concentrations of poor people, a growing number of poor single-parent families, and an increase in welfare dependency. These problems have been especially evident in the ghetto neighbourhoods of large cities, not only because the most impoverished minority populations live there, but also because the neighbourhoods have become less diversified in a way that has severely worsened the impact of the continuing economic changes.

Especially since 1970, inner-city areas have experienced an outmigration of working- and middle-class families previously confined to them by the restrictive covenants of higher-status city areas and suburbs. Combined with the increase in the number of poor caused by rising joblessness, this outmigration has sharply concentrated the poverty in inner-city areas. And the dwindling presence of middle- and working-class households in these areas has also removed an important social buffer that once deflected the full impact of the kind of prolonged high levels of joblessness in these areas that stemmed from uneven economic growth and periodic recessions.

In earlier decades, not only were most of the adults in ghetto neighbourhoods employed, but black working and middle classes brought stability. They invested economic and social resources in the neighbourhoods, patronized their churches, stores, banks and community organizations, sent their children to the local schools, reinforced conventional norms and values, and made it possible for lower-class blacks in these segregated enclaves to envision the possibility of some upward mobility.

Outmigration of the non-poor has decreased the contact between groups of different class and racial backgrounds and thereby concentrated the adverse effects of living in impoverished neighbourhoods. These 'concentration effects', reflected in a range of outcomes from degree of labour force attachment to social dispositions, are created by the constraints and opportunities that the residents of the inner-city neighbourhoods face in terms of access to jobs and job networks, involvement in quality schools, availability of marriageable partners, and exposure to conventional role models.

In short, the inner-city ghettos in large American cities feature a population, the underclass, whose primary predicament is joblessness reinforced by a growing social isolation. The vulnerability of the underclass to changes in the American economy since 1970 has resulted in sharp increases in joblessness and related problems such as welfare dependency despite the creation of anti-poverty programmes and despite anti-discrimination and affirmative action programmes.

However, throughout most of the past decade, since neither liberal nor conservative analysts of urban poverty related the fate of the urban poor to the functioning of the modern urban economy, they failed either to explain adequately or to appreciate the worsening conditions of underclass individuals, families and neighbourhoods. Conservatives erroneously attributed these problems to the social values of the ghetto poor. And liberals, slow to recognize the influence of the economy on the urban minority poor and therefore puzzled by the recent increase in inner-city social dislocations in the post-civil rights period, have lacked a convincing alternative explanation. These developments cleared the path for views on the underclass that were consistent with the dominant American belief system, views that were hardly supportive of arguments to increase the social rights of truly disadvantaged American citizens.

The quality of citizenship and the underclass

In comparison with Canada and most Western European countries, social citizenship rights in the United States are less developed and less intertwined with political and civil citizenship. Although social citizenship rights increased in the United States after the Second World War, they have yet to reach the levels enjoyed by the citizens of Western Europe. For example, American housing policies to promote home ownership have tended to benefit the working and middle classes, not the poor. 'Direct financial housing subsidies for low income families, common in European welfare states, has been virtually non-existent in the United States'.[16] The housing available for the poor tends to be confined to a limited number of public housing projects disproportionately concentrated in inner-city neighbourhoods, areas that not only lack employment opportunities but also have few informal job information networks. Moreover, Western European societies have always had a much more comprehensive programme of unemployment insurance, and the gap between the United States and Europe has widened each year since the programme lost ground in the early years of the Reagan budget. Indeed, 'in every year from 1984 through 1988 the proportion of the jobless receiving unemployment insurance benefits in an average month registered a record low. While a number of factors were at work here, including lower rates of application by eligible unemployed workers, federal and state cuts in the program played a role'.[17]

Finally, in Western European countries, where services such as medical care are considered basic collective goods, the poor tend to be covered by the same comprehensive medical programmes as the non-poor. In the United States, however, a Federal Advisory Commission recently reported that Medicaid, a health programme for poor people, pays doctors much less than either Medicare or private health insurers for the same services. As a result many doctors are refusing to take Medicaid patients.

Those at the bottom of the class structure in the United States have always suffered greater economic deprivation and insecurity.[18] The most rapid growth in expenditure on welfare programmes in the United States has been in universal entitlements such as social security, a programme of economic security for the elderly, and Medicare, a programme of health insurance for the elderly – programmes whose recipients have been mainly the working and middle classes.

Several means-tested or targeted programmes for the poor have been created in recent years but the relief provided was so minimal that they could not prevent the poor from slipping deeper into poverty. In 1975, 30 per cent of all the poor in the United States had incomes below 50 per cent of the officially designated poverty line, in 1988 40 per cent did so. Among blacks, the increase was even sharper, from 32 per cent in 1975 to nearly half (48 per cent) in 1988.[19] Moreover, the overall poverty rate actually increased after 1978. These disappointing figures are related to such factors as 'general income stagnation, the erosion of wages for lower skilled jobs in the private sector (average hourly wages were lower in real terms in 1989 than in any year since 1970), the increase in the proportion of families headed by single women, and the large decrease in real benefit levels provided by states under the [Aid for Families with Dependent Children] program'.[20]

Food stamps, Medicaid, a health programme for the poor and the supplemental security income programme (SSI) provided some relief, but, as currently designed, they have virtually no effect on the poverty rates among the non-elderly. In short, targeted programmes for the poor in the United States do not even begin to address inequities in the social class system. Instead of helping to integrate the recipients into the broader economic and social life of mainstream society, they tend to stigmatize and separate them.[21]

The lack of comprehensive programmes to promote the social rights of American citizens is especially problematic for poor inner-city blacks who are also handicapped by problems that originated in the denial of civil, political and social rights to previous generations. Although blacks had gained civil and political rights by 1970, they were not sufficient to address the problems of continued racial inequality in American society. Indeed, long periods of racial oppression can result in a system of inequality that lingers even after racial barriers come down. This is because the most disadvantaged minority individuals, crippled by the cumulative effects of both race and class subjugation (including those effects transmitted from generation to generation) are disproportionately represented among those in the total population who lack the resources to compete effectively in a free and open market.

In modern industrial society the elimination of racial barriers creates the greatest opportunities for the better-trained, talented and educated members of minority groups – those who have been least adversely affected by the system of discrimination – because they possess the most resources that enable them to compete with dominant group members for desired positions. In other words, the competitive resources possessed by the advantaged minority members – resources accruing from the family stability, financial means, peer groups and schooling that their parents have been able to provide – results in their benefiting disproportionately from policies that enhance the political and civil rights of minority individuals, policies that eliminate artificial barriers and thereby enable individuals to compete with less restraint for the more prestigious and desirable positions in society.

By the late 1960s a number of black leaders began to recognize this point. In November 1967, for example, Kenneth B. Clark stated that: 'The masses of Negroes are now starkly aware of the fact that recent civil rights victories benefited a very small percentage of middle-class Negroes while their predicament remained the same or worsened'.[22] Simply eliminating racial barriers was not going to be enough. As the late Vivian Henderson put it, 'If all racial prejudice and discrimination and all racism were erased today, all the ills brought by the process of economic class distinction and economic depression of the masses of black people would remain'.[23]

In the 1970s, as such arguments were increasingly recognized and appreciated by black leaders and liberal policy-makers, more emphasis was placed on the need not only to eliminate existing discrimination but also to counteract the effects of past racial oppression as well. Instead of seeking remedies only for individual complaints of discrimination, they sought government-mandated affirmative action programmes to ensure adequate minority representation in employment, education and public programmes. The question is to what extent did affirmative action programmes address the problem of social rights of the truly disadvantaged.

If the more advantaged members of minority groups benefit disproportionately from policies that embody the principle of equality of individual opportunity, they also profit disproportionately from policies based solely on their racial group membership. Why? Again simply because minority individuals from the most advantaged families tend to be disproportionately represented among those of their racial group most qualified for preferred positions, such as college admissions, higher-paying jobs and promotions. Thus policies of preferential treatment are likely to improve further the socioeconomic positions of the more advantaged without adequately remedying the problems of the disadvantaged. Recent data on income, employment opportunities and educational attainment suggest that only a few individuals who reside in the inner-city ghettos have benefited from affirmative action.

Thus the economically weakest members of the urban minority population have remained excluded from mainstream society. And their degree of current economic deprivation and social isolation is in part due to the limited nature of institutionalized social rights in the United States.[24] For all these reasons the effects of joblessness on the poor are far more severe than those experienced by disadvantaged groups in other advanced industrial Western societies. While economic restructuring has been common to all these societies in recent years, the most severe consequences of social and economic dislocation have been in the United States because of the underdeveloped welfare state and the weak institutional structure of social citizenship rights. Although all economically marginal groups have been affected, the black underclass has been particularly devastated because their plight has been compounded by their spatial concentration in deteriorating inner-city ghettos.

In short, the socioeconomic position of the underclass in American society is extremely precarious. The cumulative effects of historical racial exclusion have made them vulnerable to the economic restructuring of the advanced industrial economy. Moreover, the problems of joblessness, deepening poverty and other woes that have accompanied these economic changes cannot be addressed adequately by existing race-specific strategies and they are not being relieved by the meagre social rights or welfare programmes targeted at the poor. Furthermore, these problems tend to be viewed by members of the larger society as a reflection of personal deficiencies not structural inequities.

Accordingly, if any group has a stake in the enhancement of social rights in the United States, it is the ghetto underclass. Unfortunately, given the strength of the American belief system on poverty and welfare, any programme that would improve the life chances of this group would have to be based on concerns beyond those that focus on life and experiences in inner-city ghettos. Americans across racial and class boundaries continue to worry about unemployment and job security, declining real wages, escalating medical and housing costs, child care programmes, the sharp decline in the quality of public education, and crime and drug trafficking in their neighbourhoods.

These concerns are reflected in public opinion surveys. For several years national opinion polls have consistently revealed strong public backing for government labour market strategies, including training efforts, to enhance employment. A 1988 Harris poll indicated that almost three-quarters of the respondents would support a tax increase to pay for child care. A 1989 Harris poll reports that almost nine out of ten Americans would like to see fundamental change in the United States' health care system. And recent surveys conducted by the National Opinion Research Center at the University of Chicago reveal that a substantial majority of Americans want more money spent on improving the nation's educational system, and on halting rising crime and drug addiction.

The point to be emphasized, in this connection, is that programmes that increase employment opportunities and job skills training, improve public education, provide adequate child and health care, and reduce neighbourhood crime and drug abuse could alleviate many of the problems of poor minorities that cannot be successfully attacked by race-specific measures alone.

As we approach the 1990s I believe that the best political strategy for those committed to racial justice and social citizenship rights is not only to place more emphasis on race-neutral programmes to address the plight of the disadvantaged segments of the minority population, but also to discuss the application of these programmes to all groups in America, not just minorities. Indeed, an emphasis on race-neutral programmes would reinforce efforts to develop a political coalition that unites, not divides, the different racial groups; a coalition that is strong enough to push such programmes through the American Congress.

I want to emphasize that I make this recommendation because I am concerned about America's lack of commitment to the idea of equal social worth for all members of society. This recommendation goes beyond the idea of creating and effectively implementing civil rights. It also 'includes the ideal of enabling everyone to achieve full membership in the community, and to participate in what a particular society has come to regard as valued and worthwhile ways of living'.[25] In other words, a commitment to equal social worth requires that there be a safety net, 'a minimum level of resources available to everyone, sufficient to enable them to maintain a place in society'.[26] Moreover, those committed to the principle of equal social worth are much more likely to associate the problems of economic and social marginality with inequalities in the larger society not with individual deficiencies. If there were a strong commitment to equal social worth for all citizens in the United States there would be no need to discuss programmes that could uplift the minority poor in race-neutral terms. There would be support for strategies to lift the disadvantaged to an acceptable standard in modern society, regardless of racial background.

Western Europe and social citizenship reconsidered

I have suggested that there is a greater commitment to the principle of equal social worth in Western Europe than in the United States. Many observers have always resisted such comparisons, pointing out that Europe is a much more homogeneous society and that Europeans would be far less committed to this principle if they were faced with the problems of racial and cultural diversity that exist in the United States. Given the fall-out from recent economic and social changes in Europe, changes that have created problems similar to those that have plagued urban centres in the United States, there could be some merit in this argument.

In a 1977 study of the way poverty is perceived in nine Western European countries, only the United Kingdom evidenced attitudes similar to those expressed in the United States. Whereas nearly half of all the respondents to a national survey in the United Kingdom attributed poverty to 'laziness and lack of will power', only 11 per cent did so in the Federal Republic of Germany, 12 per cent in The Netherlands, 16 per cent in France, 20 per cent in Italy, 22 per cent in Belgium, 23 per cent in Denmark, and less than a third in Ireland and Luxembourg.[27] However, given the social and economic changes that have occurred in these countries since 1977, the year that study was conducted, do such attitudes hold today?

Metropolitan areas in the United States feature a much greater decentralization of businesses and selective suburbanization than those in Europe. In the past few decades, America's central cities have experienced a significant outmigration of more affluent families to the suburbs and, at the same time, a sharp increase in the number and proportion of lower income families. American metropolises have also suffered the growth of highly concentrated poverty areas or ghettos populated by millions of disadvantaged minorities.

Europe has also experienced the process of selective suburbanization but, unlike America, the city centres remain very desirable places to reside because of much better and more accessible public transport and effective urban renewal programmes. Moreover, many jobs are still being supplied by city shops and offices in European cities and, unlike the United States, cheap public transport makes suburban employment sites accessible. Also, good public education in the city centres is still much more available to the poor and disadvantaged in Europe than it is in the United States.

None the less, although they have not yet reached the degree of poverty concentration along ethnic and racial lines that is typical of metropolises in the United States, cities in Europe are developing pockets of poverty that are beginning to resemble American ghettos. For example, in Rotterdam in The Netherlands, although inner-city areas are more mixed in terms of ethnicity and social class due to extensive urban renewal, there are a number of interconnected streets or block clusters where nearly everyone is unemployed and on public assistance. These blocks resemble many ghetto streets on the South Side of Chicago or in Harlem in New York. Also in metropolitan Paris one will find a number of Algerian and African neighbourhoods that are beginning to take on the characteristics of American ghettos.

In order to understand these developments it is important to recognize that countries in Western Europe acquired a significant number of immigrants in the second half of the twentieth century. Since the late 1960s northern European economies have received workers from Turkey, the Maghreb countries of north-west Africa, northern Africa, the Middle East, and former British, Dutch and French territories. These immigrant flows have widened the cultural background differences between the immigrants and the indigenous populations.

More important, however, the economic and industrial restructuring of Europe, including the decline of traditional manufacturing areas, has decreased the need for unskilled immigrant labour. Thousands of the immigrants who had been recruited during periods of national labour shortage have been laid off by businesses.

A substantial number of the new jobs in the next few decades will require levels of training and education that are beyond the reach of most immigrant minorities. Being the last hired and the first fired, unemployment rates among immigrant minorities soared during the late 1970s through the 1980s and reached levels that ranged from 25 to 50 per cent in the cities that experienced unprecedented high levels of unemployment overall.

The creation of the single European market will very likely exacerbate not alleviate joblessness. Although the single market is expected to increase economic growth and employment opportunities substantially overall, the European Commission has warned that, initially at least, its creation could result in significant economic and social dislocations for some segments of the population, particularly the disadvantaged.

The recent economic and social changes of urban Europe have already created situations ripe for the demagogic mobilization of racism and anti-immigrant feelings. As economic conditions have worsened, many in the majority white population have viewed the growth of minorities and immigrants as part of the problem. Stagnant economies and slack labour markets in Europe have placed strains on the welfare state at the very time when the immigrant population has become more dependent on public assistance for survival.

When the European economies featured tight labour markets and economic growth the welfare state was easily financed and welfare services, with strong popular support, were either maintained or increased. However, cries to cut back on welfare programmes accompanied economic stagnation and were influenced by two developments. One was the growing costs of social service programmes and entitlement during periods of high unemployment and limited public revenues. The other was the rise to power of conservative governments in the United Kingdom and in The Netherlands, whose views about the need to cut welfare costs were buttressed by the political ascendancy of Reaganism in the United States.

In various parts of Europe ethnic and racial antagonisms have been heightened. Algerians and black Africans were attacked in several French cities and, to the dismay of French progressives, Le Pen's anti-immigrant National Front movement has experienced surprising electoral successes. Rioting occurred in several black neighbourhoods in Britain, African immigrants have been attacked in a number of Italian cities, and tensions have surfaced in several Dutch cities between Christians and Muslims and racial minorities and whites. Unfortunately, in view of the growing economic and social dislocations in Europe, expressions of overt racism, both spontaneous and organized, will be likely to increase if the economic and social problems I have thus far described are not addressed. In many respects, the Europe that we know today may not resemble the Europe we will see at the turn of the century.

As Western Europe enters a period of economic uncertainty and experiences growing problems of poverty, poverty concentration and joblessness among the disadvantaged, individuals concerned about preserving social citizenship rights should pay close attention to what has happened in urban America. I say this because there is growing convergence between Western Europe and the United States not only in the growth of ghetto neighbourhoods, but also in the way that the general public has responded to the increasing visibility and deteriorating economic and social situation of the minority and immigrant populations.

None the less, I am not convinced that the social and economic changes sweeping through Western Europe will necessarily result in sharply reduced commitments to social rights. Welfare programmes that benefit the poor, including universal welfare programmes such as child care, child allowances, housing subsidies, education and medical care are deeply institutionalized in many Western European democracies. Efforts to cut back on these programmes in the face of growing joblessness have met firm resistance. Moreover, except for England under the Thatcher government, official and scholarly explanations of the new poverty in Europe have tended to focus much more on the changes and inequities in the broader society, rather than on individual deficiencies and behaviour, and therefore lend much greater support to the ideology of equal social worth for all citizens.

However, changes in Europe are occurring very rapidly and whether the multi-racial and multi-ethnic countries there will eventually mirror the United States in both belief systems on poverty and welfare and the commitment to equal social worth is a question cross-cultural researchers are beginning to pursue with considerable interest.

Notes

This chapter is based on a larger study, *Social Isolation: Race, Class and Poverty in the Inner-City Ghetto* (Knopf, forthcoming). A shorter version of this chapter was presented at the Conference on the Quality of Citizenship, Utrecht, The Netherlands, March 1991.

1 See William Julius Wilson, *The Truly Disadvantaged: the Inner City, the Underclass and Public Policy* (University of Chicago Press, Chicago, 1987).

2 T.H. Marshall, *Class, Citizenship, and Social Development* (Doubleday, New York, 1964), p. 78.

3 James R. Kluegel and Eliot R. Smith, *Beliefs about Inequality: Americans' View of What Is and What Ought to Be* (Aldine de Gruyter, New York, 1986), p. 37.

4 Ibid.

5 For a discussion of earlier research of this kind, see James T. Patterson, *America's Struggle against Poverty, 1900–1980* (Harvard University Press, Cambridge, 1981). See also John B. Williamson, 'Beliefs about the welfare poor', *Sociology and Social Research*, 58 (January 1974), pp. 163–75; and 'Beliefs about the motivation of the poor and attitudes toward poverty policy', *Social Problems*, 21 (June 1974), pp. 634–47; and Robert H. Lauer, 'The middle class looks at poverty', *Urban and Social Change Review*, 5 (1981), pp. 8–10.

6 Robert Castel, 'The "war on poverty" and the status of poverty in an affluent society', *Actes de la recherche en sciences sociales*, 19 (January 1978), pp. 47–60.

7 Ibid., p. 47. See also Ida Susser and John Kreniski, 'The welfare trap; a public policy for deprivation', in Leith Mullings (ed.), *Cities of the United States* (Columbia University Press, New York, 1987).

8 Keith Melville and John Doble, *The Public's Perspective on Social Welfare Reform* (The Public Agenda Foundation, New York, 1988).

9 Ibid.

10 Kluegel and Smith, *Beliefs about Inequality*, pp. 37–8.

11 Melville and Doble, *The Public's Perspective*, p. x.

12 Joel Handler, *Reforming the Poor* (Basic Books, New York, 1972), p. 139.

13 Walter Korpi, 'Approaches to the study of poverty in the United States: critical notes from a European perspective', in V.T. Covello (ed.), *Poverty and Public Policy: an Evaluation of Social research* (G.K. Hall, Boston, 1980), p. 305.

14 Ibid, pp. (emphasis added).

15 Melville and Doble, *The Public's Perspective*, p. 3.

16 Barbara Schmitter-Heisler, 'A comparative perspective on the underclass: questions of urban poverty, race and citizenship'. Paper presented at the Annual Meeting of the Eastern Sociological Society, Baltimore, MD, 17–19 March 1989, p. 10.

17 Robert Greenstein, 'Universal and targeted approaches to relieving poverty: an alternative view', in Christopher Jencks and Paul Peterson (eds), *The Urban Underclass* (Brookings Institutions Press, Washington DC, 1991), pp. 399–440.

18 Schmitter-Heisler, 'A comparative perspective'.

19 US Bureau of the Census, 'Money income and poverty status in the US (Table 2)', in *Current Population Reports, Series P-60* (Government Printing Office, Washington, DC, 1988).

20 Greenstein, 'Universal and targeted approaches'.

21 Schmitter-Heisler, 'A comparative perspective'.

22 Kenneth B. Clark, 'The present dilemma of the negro'. Paper presented at the Annual Meeting of the Southern Regional Council (Atlanta, GA, 2 November 1967), p. 8.

23 Vivian Henderson, 'Race, economic and public policy', *Crisis*, 82 (1975), pp. 50–5.

24 Schmitter-Heisler, 'A comparative perspective'.

25 J. Donald Moon, 'The moral basis of the democratic welfare state', in Amy Gutmann (ed.), *Democracy and the Welfare State* (Princeton University Press, Princeton, NJ, 1988), pp. 53–78.

26 Ibid., p. 43.

27 Commission of the European Community, *The Perception of Poverty in Europe* (EEC, Brussels, 1977).

6

CITIZENSHIP, WORK AND WELFARE

Hans Adriaansens

According to T.H. Marshall, the notion of citizenship triggered development towards welfare state provision in the Western world. During the twentieth century citizenship notions have centred around the social (instead of the civil and political) dimensions of life and have resulted in a welfare state which has brought an unparalleled level of material independence to its individual citizens.

Since the 1980s, however, this seemingly unidirectional development towards more individual and material independence has slowed down and in some cases even reversed. All over the Western world welfare states have come under financial and ideological pressure. Social security benefits – the hallmark of social citizenship – expanded to such an extent that the security they brought crumbled under the growing volume of beneficiaries. Many of the welfare states of the West were not able anymore to keep up their social promises. They allowed growing groups of citizens to become excluded from the main processes of societal life. Massive unemployment is a case in point. At the same time, the welfare state came under ideological criticism as well: it became identified with an all-powerful state that stultifies the individual citizen, taking away the freedom for personal initiative. History, we know, can sometimes be cruel: by becoming free of its citizenship base, the welfare state has come under the very fire it was designed to extinguish . . .

From both a financial and an ideological point of view it is about time to formulate a reappraisal of the chances for a serious welfare state. The notion of citizenship plays an important part in such a reappraisal. In this chapter I shall argue that a more active implementation of citizenship by way of creating a participatory structure (instead of concentrating merely on the moral level of individual and 'passive' social security rights) will form the ticket under which the welfare state can embark on a new future. On the foundation of a basic level of social security, the welfare state should rather develop a social and economic structure of chances. The discussion about citizenship has thus far been a discussion about rights and obligations. It is about time that this discussion went beyond the 'moral' level and turned to the social structural prerequisites underlying the moral discourse.

Welfare state and citizenship

Rethinking the welfare state means the reappraisal of thinking and doing about work and welfare. Work and welfare are the twin pillars on which the edifice of the welfare state has been constructed. Thinking and doing stand for the ways in which professionals and politicians have gone about furnishing that building. The direction of the change may best be characterized as follows: the traditional welfare state was intended as a safety net for those who were in danger of losing their economic autonomy. This safety net function remains uncontested. A minimum standard of living is ensured by means of employment, disability benefits, the old age pension and various other social security benefits. As time has gone by, however, the safety net of the welfare state has evolved into a snare; citizens 'caught' by the net run the risk of becoming entangled in its strands. This is not only lamentable in itself but it also contributes to the danger that the safety net function can no longer be sustained at the desired level. The last, the lost, the least and the latest may evolve into what is termed in modern literature on poverty the 'underclass'. The task for the 'new' welfare state is therefore to arrange the safety net in such a way that it acts for most citizens not as a snare but as a trampoline providing them with a soft landing and a fresh chance of establishing a place in society.

The fact that the welfare state should be subject to growing reappraisal at this precise time is not surprising. While the problems may go back to an earlier date, it takes time to escape the embrace of a successful 'discourse'. And the discourse of the welfare state has undeniably been successful for a long time, to the point that in the critical area of work and welfare 'thinking and doing' have evolved into an almost closed system. This system has its own dynamics and its own criteria for assessing the good and the bad, the suitable and the unsuitable, and the true and the false. However great their self-perceived antithesis may be, social science and political practice are often so closely intertwined as to reinforce one another for better or for worse. The room for new kinds of critical appraisal arise only when thinking and doing regularly and overtly come into conflict and see reality slipping from their grasp.

There can be no doubt that we currently find ourselves in such a situation. The paradoxes of the welfare state – the paradoxes of work and welfare – are becoming increasingly conspicuous. A few examples may suffice. From a socioeconomic perspective it is notable that unemployment and labour shortages exist side by side; that efforts to combat unemployment often take forms which serve to reduce the labour force participation rate, e.g. early retirement and disability schemes; that various welfare states in the West tend to combine a low participation rate with a high level of productivity; that they also combine a high standard of health with a high degree of employment disability; that the drive for efficiency in the formal labour circuit is coupled with an undisguised cultivation of the informal or voluntary circuit; and that benefits are not just expressions of social justice but often also act as a pay-off for socially deployable energy.

The cycle of rising social security expenditure, higher wage costs, downward pressure on employment, upward pressure on labour productivity and the higher rate of exit from the labour force under the unemployment, early retirement and employment disability regulations is characteristic of the evolution of the welfare state in the 1970s and 1980s. Since then the upturn in the economy has slowed this downward spiral. This has not, however, solved the problem of the welfare state: it continues to make heavy weather as it has proved difficult to hold down the budget deficit. Cuts in government spending appear to have evolved into an intrinsic element of the welfare state. At the same time the spending cuts have created new paradoxes: for the debate about present-day poverty reflects a harsh reality and cannot be brushed under the carpet.

Work and welfare

Work and welfare are the central dimensions of the welfare state and also provide the coordinates for the social position of its citizens. Regulations with respect to work and welfare have evolved over a long period of time and are an expression of deeply cherished convictions. It is therefore worth considering these underlying principles in a little more detail.

The origins of the welfare state go back far into history. For our purposes, however, it is sufficient to look back to the 1950s and

1960s and therefore to the highwater mark of an economy in which work was to a much greater extent 'labour' than it is now, and in which this very 'labour' element was neutralized by a religiously inspired work ethic. At the same time the organization of employment focused primarily on the family, in which the breadwinner acted as intermediary; there was little if any focus on the individual citizen. When the welfare state established itself in the 1950s and 1960s it did so on these two basic foundations:

1   A dominant industrial economy, underpinned by a religiously inspired work ethic.
2   A dominant family philosophy, in which the breadwinner was responsible for the economic independence of the family household and his partner for the family's well-being.

'Full employment' formed the socioeconomic policy translation of these foundations. In many Western countries it became the principal objective of official socioeconomic policy. In the light of the above principles, however, it will be evident that full employment was achieved in the 1960s at a comparatively low labour force participation rate. In The Netherlands, for example, a mere 59 per cent of the population aged 15–65 had jobs during this period of full employment. 'Guestworkers' were recruited from the Mediterranean region in order to ease the shortages in the labour market. In other words, the socioeconomic concept of full employment was subject to a sociocultural limit, in the sense that the principles outlined above made it impossible for women to enter the labour force in large numbers.

As far as Holland is concerned, the trend was in fact in the opposite direction. In the early 1950s many felt that the social and economic reconstruction of the Netherlands was proceeding too slowly. For many young people this provided grounds for exchanging the certainty of a meagre existence for the uncertainties, opportunities and promises of an existence in regions that had been less affected by the war and where willingness to work hard would eventually be rewarded in hard cash. Young families ventured out to Canada and Australia without any illusions but that they would face hard work. Men had to take on everything and women too would have no opportunity to sit still. Apart from caring for their ever growing number of offspring women also had to do their bit to make ends meet. When the contours of the Dutch welfare state began to take shape during the 1950s the news naturally reached Canada and Australia. The stories of emigrants who had been 'back', generally on account of some family misfortune, were plain: the Netherlands had become a prosperous country – so prosperous that women did not even have to work outside the home! Women, according to these travel stories, were simply required to look after their families while their husbands earned a living. Many migrant families decided at that time to turn their backs on their 'country of the future' and to return to the Netherlands – where the future had already become reality.

This example shows that the marriage between the traditional economy and family philosophy was also confirmed by a social security system which was to protect as many as possible against the hardships of economic production.

In the meantime the signposts have moved, which is, of course, hardly surprising. For no social order can expect to hold out against the tide of history. The prosperity of Western countries is no longer measured in terms of the opportunity for women to withdraw from the labour market. On the contrary: for women too, particularly for the younger generations, the chance to work outside the home has now become a sign of emancipation and independence.

This reversal is worth considering in more detail. What has happened in the meantime? Essentially, the two main foundations of yester-year have been attacked. The economy has been restructured on a grand scale: automation and the technological and information revolutions have converted the predominantly industrial economies into post-industrial ones. Apart from the agricultural and industrial sectors, tertiary and quaternary 'service' sectors have evolved, which in many Western welfare countries have risen to two-thirds of total employment. Changes in the attitude towards work as well as changes in the demand for labour have resulted from this: increasingly it is the better educated and trained workers who are required, while those lacking training run an ever-growing risk of becoming detached from the process of economic production.

Similarly, the welfare pillar has been shaken in the past two decades. Both the traditional family philosophy and the religiously inspired work ethic have changed radically. The process of individualization has resulted in smaller families, created new forms of primary relationships and led to a sharp increase in the number of one-person households. Groups that formerly gave no thought to entering the labour market and which were therefore not particularly concerned about their education now wish to turn their training to practical account. In this respect the claim for economic independence undoubtedly plays a greater role than does the traditional work ethic.

These two structural developments – the restructuring of the economy and the process of individualization – have shaken the traditional pillars of the welfare state and should therefore have led to 'fundamental' adjustments in good time. But so solidly and firmly was the edifice built that it proved capable of remaining upright despite its shifting foundations. Gradually, however, the foundations suffered further erosion and the cracks in the structure became larger and more conspicuous. This led to the reappraisals of the 1980s, summarized under the notion of 'Thatcherism' in England and 'no-nonsense-politics' in the Netherlands. But these reviews did not address the key issue of the welfare state, namely the need for a new link between work and welfare, a link that takes account of the changes in the economy on the one hand and in household formation on the other. The most important element in this new link consists in a higher and better labour force participation. But before going into detail, I shall devote some time to the ways in which social science and practical politics have hindered the welfare state from coming to grips with its fundamentally changed environment.

Thinking and doing

Earlier I defined the latest citizenship impulse in the welfare state as 'a reappraisal of thinking and doing with respect to work and welfare'. While I have addressed the subject of work and welfare I have so far had little to say about thinking and doing – or social science and political practice. For it has not only been the institutions surrounding work and welfare that have hampered the adjustment of the welfare state to new developments. These institutions have been able to survive as long as they have because they were underpinned by a number of implicit and hence also 'self-evident' basic propositions, two of which are examined below.

Over the past few decades one particular notion, which has established itself in both social science and political practice, has rendered an open debate about a new link between work and welfare virtually impossible. That notion concerns the relationship between the economic and the social; or, in academic terms, the relationship between economic and social rationality. In varying guises, social science maintains that economic rationality is increasingly penetrating the social sphere; that the 'system' is beginning to dominate and even 'colonize' the human 'life-world'; that 'functional' or 'technical rationality' is increasingly displacing 'substantial rationality'; that 'meaning' is superseded by 'function'; and that the private sphere of the family has come to act in the public domain as a 'haven in a heartless world'.

In themselves, there is nothing wrong with these notions and the ideas behind them. But the question to arise from this self-evident consensus is by nature of a conservative kind, however progressively it may sometimes be formulated, namely: 'How can the attack of economic on social rationality be held in check, stopped and even reversed? How can a barrier be erected against the flood of economic primacy?' Projected onto employment and the labour market the question has received the answers it has sought: proposals for a basic income, a widely supported leisure ideology, a highly elaborated social security system, the gradual 'normalization' of unemployment, a huge informal circuit and an emphatic call for and cultivation of the deployment of voluntary unpaid labour. Economically, these 'answers' necessarily resulted in an increase in gross wage costs, a further increase in the pressure on efficient production by an ever-decreasing segment of the population, higher levels of unemployment, and in general the gradual weakening of the economic and entrepreneurial climate. Socially the result has been the continuation of inadequate attention to the quality of employment and, paradoxically, sticking to old nineteenth-century standards of what labour is all about.

A second, related propositon concerns the role and value of labour in the overall pattern of social participation and citizenship. The typical welfare state attitude towards employment may without exaggeration be regarded as one of marked reserve. The link with the industrial age and the physical 'labour' characteristic of that time has consistently shone through. Instead of a full-blown sign of citizenship, work was a cross that had to be borne; genuine well-being had to be sought elsewhere, in leisure for example. Without question this attitude has also operated as a self-fulfilling prophecy and ensured that the labour nature of employment held sway for much longer than necessary.

In terms of renewing the welfare state into a participatory structure it is necessary to close rather than widen the gap between the economic and the social as well as to debunk the alleged antithesis of economic and social participation. Of much greater interest than this opposition is the question as to how on earth it should be possible that, despite all the changes in the nature of both work and household formation, so little of these have so far penetrated into the organization of the labour market. Does not the real problem reside in the fact that, by our very attempts at keeping 'the system' outside, aspects of social or substantial rationality have not succeeded in penetrating this system of economic rationality except to a rather limited extent? In more concrete terms: why are there so few work-related facilities for child care, for flexible pension arrangements, for recurrent employment, for recurrent education? Particularly at a time in which the binding force of traditional integrative linkages – from family to church – are subject to erosion, the positive linkage of formal employment, individual citizenship and social integration puts a great emphasis on the importance of labour force participation. It has become an increasingly important means of filling the gap between economic 'system' and social 'life'.

Labour force participation: policy measures

Reference to the structural prerequisites of a system of social citizenship adapted to the times means penetrating to the institutional heart of the traditional welfare state. For the institutional setting upon which the welfare arrangements of the 1950s and 1960s could flourish now prevent the modern welfare state from adapting to new circumstances.

However prosaic it may sound, it is in the wage structure or the system of wage formation that the post war attitudes about work and welfare took institutional shape. In many Western countries, wages were primarily geared to breadwinner households. In some countries this resulted in fixing the minimum wage at a level sufficient to maintain a family with two children. Similarly, the family philosophy played an important role in the discussion as to whether men and women should receive equal pay for equal work. The division of responsibilities between men and women and between breadwinners and their dependents was such a basic aspect of the social system that women engaged in the labour process received 'separate' treatment.

In the meantime the situation has changed radically. In The Netherlands, for example, only 0.4 per cent (!) of all employees at the minimum wage level have to maintain a family household. Most minimum wages are earned by single householders aged under 27 or in households in which the minimum wage is not the sole source of income. The original conception of the minimum wage has been overtaken by the individualization process.

Individualization of the wage structure is therefore a sensible policy strategy that is consistent with the changes in the economy and society. As this strategy will have consequences, particularly at the lower regions of the wage structure, it may also contribute to improving both the employment situation at the unskilled level and the entrepreneurial climate for 'starters'. By creating greater room at the bottom of the wage structure (under the condition, of course, that workers who do have to maintain a family can call on supplementary regulations) a serious effort can be made to create new jobs (e.g. by job-splitting), while tasks (or elements of tasks) currently handled solely in the informal labour circuit can be brought into the formal circuit. This would mean that a large number of relatively unproductive tasks would be returned to the formal circuit.

A second element in a policy which by promoting labour force participation fulfils a prerequisite for social citizenship relates to strengthening an 'active labour market policy'. The bulk of governmental labour market funding has taken the form of benefits which are comparatively 'passive' in nature and have no activating effect on the recipients of these benefits. This did not pose a problem in the 1960s, when only small numbers of people were obliged to resort to benefits. But during the 1980s the system of unemployment benefits also functioned as a regular source of economic independence, thereby consolidating itself and frustrating the ability of the formal circuit to develop. It has become important that parallel to a policy which strengthens the demand-side of the labour market, the supply-side also develops activating stimuli which can bring people (back) into the labour market.

Any suggestion that the system of education can continue indefinitely as it has done in recent decades fails to take account of the qualitative changes that have taken place in economy and society. The implicit notion that the vocational qualifications of a person entering the labour force at the age of 20 remain unchanged until that person retires at 65 has been overtaken by events, as the redundancy figures make clear. Both the process of economic production and the employees in question have an increasing need for mobility, change and adaptation to altered circumstances. A system of 'recurrent education' is therefore essential.

Such a system would need to consist of a number of elements. In the first place facilities would need to be provided to enable unskilled workers to obtain some basic form of qualification. The same should apply to the unemployed and the returners. Secondly, all those with a basic qualification but lacking work should be given the opportunity of pursuing vocational courses. Finally, employees should be provided with the opportunity at one or several points in their careers of interrupting their employment for the purposes of further training or retraining. Next to this system of 'recurrent education' a system of 'recurrent employment' should enable people to coordinate their private and work situations more effectively. Particularly important in this respect are regulations relating to parental leave, in the sense of ensuring that the care of the family with young children does not necessarily lead to the loss of one's job. Such arrangements can also help bring about a more equal distribution of the 'caring' tasks within a household.

In the meantime many of the elderly are also no longer so willing to accept an abrupt and also premature termination of their careers as inevitable. Two contrary movements may be discerned in this respect. On the one hand, there is a growing group of elderly people who are both mentally and physically prepared for and capable of performing meaningful work up to an advanced age. On the other hand, the development of the economy has led to a substantial decline in labour force participation in the 1970s and 1980s for precisely the category of those aged over 50. Opening up possibilities for 'second careers' with less exacting productivity requirements would make a sensible type of policy in this respect. A major obstacle, however, is that in many countries pension arrangements are geared to final pay. Dropping a rung would therefore also mean that an element of accumulated pension entitlements was lost. It would therefore be worth examining the adjustment of these pension schemes. In addition, the possibility of introducing flexible pension arrangements deserves further study.

In the case of women, the further individualization of income tax could serve to increase their labour participation. In many countries the system of taxation reflects the traditional breadwinner philosophy, whereby tax allowances were given to working husbands. Although understandable during the 1950s and 1960s, this very system now develops into a barrier for labour force participation, as international comparative studies show.

These are just a few examples of how socioeconomic policies can bring about the participatory conditions for a social citizenship adapted to the times. The problem, however, is that these policies not only seem to attack time-honoured principles of yester-year, but also require joint action of governmental agencies, employers' organizations and labour unions. The road to such joint action is strewn with mines as the logic of micro-rationality differs greatly from that of macro-rationality. Traditional welfare states have succeeded in bridging this gap for quite a while. 'Market' and 'plan', individual preferences and macro-planning, worked well in each other's interests. Social citizenship and welfare state were, as Marshall stated and Keynes implied, the two sides of this coin. Now that the dynamics of development have changed the underlying structure, it may come as no surprise that both citizenship and welfare state are jeopardized. In this situation, a choice between citizenship and welfare state is not required. What we need is a system of macro-planning which stimulates and provokes the market of entrepreneurial and independent citizens. In this new situation socioeconomic considerations should play the same important part as they played in the 1950s and 1960s. The content of these considerations, however, should be geared to the conditions of the 1990s.

7

MARRIAGE AND THE BOUNDARIES OF CITIZENSHIP

Ursula Vogel

> Marriage has a long history, and we live in its shadow.
> (Susan Okin, *Justice, Gender, and the Family*)

In reflecting on the nature of citizenship in contemporary liberal democracies we frequently make use of the phrase 'second-class citizens'. This is a curious term. It suggests that membership of a political community is both universal and hierarchically ordered. The lower ranks in this order will typically include ethnic minorities, immigrants, poor and disabled people – and women. As far as the law is concerned, the individuals belonging to such groups are recognized as full members of the community. Yet they are, in many important respects, treated as if they were not.

What is the nature of those class divisions that run through the allegedly homogeneous terrain of modern citizenship? How can we account for the barriers and distances which separate second-class citizens from master citizens? We might say that differences of colour, ethnicity and sex, although they have long been removed from the formal, legal qualifications of citizen status, still have some purchase in the informal mechanisms of our political culture. Or, we might refer to the specific disadvantages suffered by these groups as latecomers to the political arena. They often lack the resources that are necessary to make full use of the equal entitlements and opportunities postulated in the idea of democratic citizenship. Money, time, health, education, command of the dominant language, as well as organization and connections within the spheres of institutionalized power – all these factors could be listed among the assets without which the avenues to effective citizen participation will remain closed.

But an account which merely identifies particular disadvantages in this way is inadequate. It omits a crucial dimension, namely that second-class citizens bear the burden of a long history of dependence and subordination. They have, to put it differently, not been altogether excluded from the story of modern citizenship. They have been part of it, but as subjects and subordinates of citizens. Neither the one-dimensional language of exclusion and inclusion, nor a catalogue of privileges and liabilities alone will capture the nature of those relationships that once connected citizens and non-citizens in a nexus of rule and subservience. In the case of women, the legacies of dependence, of prolonged tutelage and submission to the rule of men are encapsulated in the history of marriage.

Political theory has had little to say about the relationship between the institution of marriage and the status of individuals in the public spaces of a democratic polity. The dominant paradigm that has served to explain the historical evolution of modern citizenship has claimed a much impeded, yet inexorable, thrust towards universal citizen status. From the Archimedean point of completed universality women's peculiar place in this history can be found in the categories of exclusion and merely delayed emancipation. It can be rendered invisible in the generous allowance made for historical anomalies in an otherwise regular process of democratization.[1]

What, however, is lost in such accounts is the paradoxical nexus of exclusion and inclusion (of universality and particularity, of equality and *Herrschaft*) which lies at the heart of modern ideas of citizenship. Universal definitions of citizen status have not, in a merely contingent manner, run alongside assertions of normative particularity in the relations of marriage. They cannot even be understood without reference to a supporting cast of significant differences. Carole Pateman's retrieval of the 'sexual contract' as the hidden part of the story told in classical social contract doctrines has shown that women, as wives, were not excluded from the original constitution of political society. They were incorporated in it – as the subordinates of men.[2] Pateman's interpretation emphasizes, above all, the division between a sphere of private power and privilege, on the one hand, and a public domain of equal political agency, on the other. The argument of this chapter will focus on the non-private, overtly political meanings of marriage as a nexus of domination and subjection.

The next section will consider two dominant strands in the history of legal and political thought. We shall see, first, how closely natural law doctrines of the seventeenth and eighteenth centuries linked the universal foundations of modern citizenship to the hierarchical order of marriage. The second example, taken from de Tocqueville's account of American democracy, will emphasize the peculiar dialectic of freedom and subordination in nineteenth-century liberal conceptions of democratic citizenship. This example, too, will show that women's place in the history of citizenship cannot be explained by the contingent factors that adhere to historical anomalies, or by the effects of a merely delayed process of emancipation. De Tocqueville and many liberal thinkers of his time – John Stuart Mill was a notable exception – entrusted the autocratic regime of marriage with the distinctly modern function of counteracting the much feared disruptive forces of unbounded social equality. The concluding section will review different perspectives from which feminist theory today has analysed and evaluated the historical legacies of falsely universalist citizenship.

In charting the ways in which the divides of gender have affected the universal conditions of citizenship, I shall talk about marriage as an 'institution'. I shall concentrate, that is, on relations of power created and sustained by the law. People often identify the law with a body of abstract rules, with formal arrangements and technical meanings which, as such, bear but little on the concrete facets of social experience. However, as we shall see with regard to marriage, the concepts and images in which the law expresses the normative principles of an institution circulate not only in legislative committees and courtrooms. They are part of a common language that reflects and shapes a society's collective values and perceptions.[3] And it is because such representations of a legal order are rooted in the many layers of a political culture that the institutions to which they refer have often proved so resilient to change.

Equality and *Herrschaft* in marriage

> There can exist no obligation demanding obedience from a wife before she has by her own consent submitted to the will of her husband.
>
> (Samuel Pufendorf, *Acht Bücher vom Natur- und Völkerrechte*)

The history of European marriage laws, from the Middle Ages until well into the twentieth century, records the extensive range and the tangible form of those special powers which allowed a husband to control the body, property and freedom of his wife.[4] European legal systems conveyed the nature of this power in different analogies: as *Geschlechtsvormundschaft* (marital guardianship); as *puissance maritale* (with its resonances of the Roman *patria potestas*); as feudal bondage (in the nexus of *baron and feme* under the English Common law). The relationship between husband and wife mirrored the bonds between superior and inferior, ruler and subject. While in the legal order of the medieval period all social relations conformed to principles of hierarchy and ascribed status, modern legal doctrines since the seventeenth century assumed the abstract equality of all individuals as legal agents. By the end of the nineteenth century, marriage alone (if we exempt the special case of paternal power over children) had retained some of the peculiar attributes of feudal bondage. It had remained a status relationship in which a husband, *qua* husband, had certain proprietory rights to the person of his wife. Long after the abolition of slavery and feudal servitude, after the emancipation of the Jews and the recognition of the civil status of aliens, women, as wives, still lacked some of the basic attributes of autonomous legal agency. Deprived of full property rights in her person and labour, of contractual capacities and independent access to justice, a wife stood in no direct relation to the state and its law. Conversely, the husband's rights of command as well as his obligations of protection and representation had a distinctly public dimension. He was citizen and ruler in one person.

How could a relationship reminiscent of feudal bondage still be justified in 'modern' philosophical doctrines? What could accord legitimacy to an institution which was so clearly at odds with the universalist postulates of individual right and of obligation based solely upon consent? In the systematic deduction of rights and duties, of property, contract and legitimate authority from the single source of secular reason, modern natural law in the tradition of Grotius, Hobbes and Pufendorf established the legal foundations of universal citizenship.[5] It developed the normative framework of those rights which, in Marshall's formulation, constitute the first, civil rights dimension of citizen status.

Natural jurisprudence conceived of civil society as a unified system of contractual associations which ranged from the *societas conjugalis* (conjugal society), at one end of the spectrum, to the political constitution of a people under government, at the other. Legitimate power in all of society's institutions followed from the single and homogeneous principle of valid contractual procedures. In this evolution of modern legal philosophy, marriage occupied a position of paradigmatic significance. Politically, it was the institution in whose terrain the competing claims of church and state struggled for supremacy. Epistemologically, marriage provided the experimental field for the philosophical intention to shift the foundations of moral and political knowledge from the prescriptions of divine law to the imperatives of self-sufficient human reason. To remove marriage from the doctrinal and jurisdictional supremacy of the Church by incorporating it in the normative structure of ordinary civil contracts was to dispute all claims to political authority made on behalf of religious dogma.[6]

To legitimate this transfer, natural law thinkers have to argue not only that the conditions of a valid marriage derive from the consent of the individual parties (a requirement already well established by the Canon law). The logic of contractual procedures has to be seen to apply also to the internal order of marriage and to the construction of conjugal rights and duties. Divested of any pre-established sacramental or metajuridical status the obligations of husband and wife can thus be considered legitimate only if they result from an agreement between two contracting agents of equal standing. Neither the legacy of Eve's culpability nor the head–body metaphor of the Scriptures can any longer provide sufficient reasons for subordinating the wife to the husband. Nothing but her own voluntary submission will satisfy the epistemological demands on the stringent derivation of legitimate power.[7] However, as they move to a lower level of abstraction where the concrete institutional implications of those principles have to be spelt out, natural law doctrines reinstate the husband's conjugal right as if it were the indisputable prerequisite of any social order.

The tension between the general principle of equality and the perceived demands of order and stability has, of course, been a persistent feature in all discussions of citizenship. This conflict of principles has, however, affected marriage in a particular way, and it is important to understand its peculiar historical origins. The emphasis on 'order' has little to do with the demands on a wife's domestic duties. Her subordination is not justified by the need of forcing her to attend to the care of household and children. Rather, the task at hand is to construe a power that will secure the unity of marriage, as well as the tranquillity of civil society, against the adverse consequences of a wife's independence of will. But why should women be the particular target of this concern with order and disorder? What does the social order have to be protected against? What, indeed, is the meaning of 'order' and 'disorder'? The predominant motif for committing women to the strictest rules of obedience and submission must be sought in the belief that only the coercive sanctions of the law will enable a husband to ensure the sexual fidelity of his wife. This assumption runs as a persistent theme through legal arguments from the seventeenth to the nineteenth centuries. The meanings of citizenship, of legitimate authority, of the purposes of the state did, of course, change considerably over this period. What persists, as we shall see from the example of de Tocqueville, is the ghost of women's independence and the spectre of anarchy that it evokes. From Pufendorf to Montesquieu, Rousseau and the framers of the Code Napoléon political thinkers and jurists postulate a causal chain that connects the preservation of civil society over time with the undisturbed passage of property along family lineages and, hence, the guaranteed certainty of biological fatherhood.[8] Hobbes' state of nature as the paradigm of uncertainty has its close if much less discussed equivalent in Pufendorf's and Rousseau's vision of the calamities that will afflict a society where nobody can know for certain 'whether citizens descended from a legitimate marriage or adultery'.[9] Nothing less than the permanence of the legal order and, indeed, the immortality of civil society are staked upon the presumption 'that every child can be considered the son of the mother's husband'.[10]

The need to enforce this presumption was the explicit purpose of the adultery laws which in most European legal systems lasted into the twentieth century. These laws treated the infidelity of a wife by altogether different standards and punishments than the same offence committed by a husband.[11] The salient point for our argument is the coercive yet, according to a long tradition of political philosophy, 'legitimate' nature of the power to which a wife was subjected. The many instances in which the husband could legitimately restrict her freedom (freedom of domicile, of travel, of disposal over property, of work and sociability) made him master over the physical space in which she moved. The law thus empowered him to constrain her liberty in the most tangible sense of the word in order, ultimately, to protect his right of exclusive access to her body. As we have seen, however, personal power of this kind was already in the seventeenth century no longer capable of consistent legitimation. Nor could a compelling case have been made on the basis of empirical observation and experience. There was no evidence to suggest that a weakening of the husband's imperium would prompt an epidemic of female adultery and the subsequent descent of civil society into chaos. Philosophical argument and empirical facts alike were overlayed by powerful and, no doubt, widely held beliefs which converted the image of women's independence into apocalyptic visions of social disorder. It is against the background of this history that the conditions of women's second-class citizenship have to be assessed.

Democratic citizenship and domestic hierarchy: de Tocqueville's America

> . . . and in the United States one never hears an adulterous wife noisily proclaiming the rights of women while stamping the most hallowed duties under foot.
>
> (Alexis de Tocqueville, *Democracy in America*)

In the much changed political and intellectual environment of de Tocqueville's account of American democracy we can still observe a similar correlation between the conditions of a well-ordered polity, on the one hand, and the necessity of imposing strict constraints upon the freedom of the married woman, on the other.[12] This normative asymmetry between the two orders of marriage and the state is, however, cast into the distinct language of democratic citizenship. De Tocqueville claimed the unquestionable authority of the husband over the wife and the strictest seclusion of the latter in the sphere of domestic duties as one of the main reasons why the American experiment in democracy had been uniquely successful:

> Nor have the Americans ever supposed that democratic principles should undermine the husband's authority and make it doubtful who is in charge of the family . . . Thus, then, while they have allowed the social inferiority of woman to continue, they have done everything to raise her morally and intellectually to the level of man. In this I think they have wonderfully understood the true conception of democratic progress.[13]

Democratic principles are, on this reading, not incompatible with a marriage premised upon marital power. On the contrary, the latter complements and sustains the former. In Europe, 'the crude, disorderly fancy of our age' has led to absurd notions of equality between the sexes which 'would attribute the same functions to both, impose the same duties and grant the same rights; they would have them share everything – work, pleasure, public affairs'.[14] In America, the principle of social equality has eroded the distinctions of social rank and ascribed status but has found its natural limit in the relationship between husband and wife. While thus claiming the complementarity of marriage and the political order, de Tocqueville, in fact, affirms the medieval structures of the English Common law as the requisite of a modern egalitarian order. He is not, however, concerned to underwrite the sacredness of a traditional institution. Nor does he in any way assume the natural weakness or natural inferiority of the female sex. He dwells with enthusiasm on the considerable independence and on the high standard of education which distinguish the status of the young unmarried woman in America. As long as she lives in her father's house she enjoys freedom and sociability. For the married woman, by contrast, the husband's abode 'is almost a cloister'.[15] This transition, de Tocqueville argues, comes about as a result of unconstrained choice. At the threshold of matrimony the American woman is said to freely submit to the 'yoke' of life-long submission. Not natural submissiveness motivates her to thus renounce her freedom, but strength of character, self-conscious virtue and self-willed sacrifice.

That in the status of the married woman bondage will shade into freedom is, above all, due to the fact that de Tocqueville does not view democracy and democratic citizenship primarily from the perspective of formal rights and constitutional mechanisms. In order to flourish, democracy requires more than an appropriate legal and institutional framework. It must be rooted in the wider political culture of the nation – in its *moeurs* (mores). Mores encompass religious and economic practices, the organization of family and neighbourhood, and the strength of citizen involvement in voluntary associations. This fabric of social morality which has to sustain a democratic constitution depends, in turn, on the virtue of women. It is they who, without being citizens themselves, guard a democratic society against the dangers inherent in democracy. 'There have never been free societies without mores, and . . . it is woman who shapes these mores. Therefore everything which has a bearing on the status of women, their habits, and their thoughts is, in my view, of great political importance.'[16]

At first sight de Tocqueville's account seems to aim at a functional correlation between the enclosed world of female virtue and the public sphere of men's citizenship. But the claimed complementarity – and equal value – of the two spheres is fraught with serious contradictions. That in a society where most men devote themselves to business or a political career women should attend to the tasks of the household is one thing. That in order to perform those duties they should be locked away, as it were, behind the walls of a convent, is quite another. Similarly, great emphasis is placed upon the egalitarian sentiments of American society and on the ways in which the Americans have transformed the authoritarian structures of familial relations into bonds of mutual respect and affection. But if husband and wife have thus become companions, why should it be necessary that women submit to the 'yoke' of marriage, i.e. to a power backed by legal sanctions? Why should public opinion in a democracy demand that the married woman be 'imprisoned' in the narrow circle of domestic duties? The emphasis on the legal ties of marriage accords neither with the stability functions of this institution nor with the beneficial complementarity of male and female character. It accords least of all with any notion of moral autonomy.

'In America a woman loses her independence for ever in the bonds of matrimony.'[17] How can we explain the language of enforced seclusion and legally ascribed subordination which continuously intrudes upon the language of freedom? We need to distinguish several strands of motivation behind an argument that asserts the unique 'political' significance of women to the well-being of democracy and, at the same time and 'for ever', seals the boundaries of democratic citizenship against their right of inclusion. First, like many liberals of his time, de Tocqueville links the freedom and equality of citizens in the public domain to the conditions of autocratic government in the household and, in particular, to the unquestionable authority of husbands over wives. The belief that, unlike despotic government, a republic owes its strength to the purity of manners among its citizens recalls the example of classical antiquity. The exclusion of women from the public spaces of the ancient polis would have been an integral part of these powerful memories.

The heritage of classical republicanism is, secondly, reinforced by the specifically modern perceptions of a precarious balance between democracy and order. De Tocqueville's positive evaluation of democratic principles – and the same can be said of much liberal thought in the nineteenth century – is overcast by the apprehensions of a 'liberalism of fear'.[18] Such perceptions focus on the anarchic, self-destructive tendencies that might be unleashed by the process of democratization and on the intrinsic vulnerability of a democratic order to the subversive dynamic of equality. Hence the insistence that democracy as a levelling principle of ultimately uncontrollable power must be complemented and contained by havens of unchallenged authority. The institutional fixation of sexual difference in the hierarchical marriage is to protect democratic society against an understanding of equality that would break down all distinctions and meaningful differences.

Thirdly, the paradoxical nexus of citizenship and bondage, of companionship and subordination is, here too, rooted in the belief that the stability of political society requires the guarantee of sexual fidelity. Unlike the writers discussed in the previous section, de Tocqueville applies the imperatives of chastity to both men and women. He emphatically condemns the double standard of adultery still so prevalent in his time. Indeed, he attributes to women and their traditional role a superior power to uphold society's sexual morality. We might say that it is still the same theme which justifies women's seclusion in the bonds of marriage by the demands of sexual purity. But embedded in positive meanings their absence from the public arena will accord more easily with the sensibilities of a democratic culture. The boundaries of citizenship are thus rendered more acceptable – and more resistant to change.

Natural law doctrines of the seventeenth and eighteenth centuries emphasized the need for placing tangible constraints upon the freedom of the married woman. They left no doubt that the relationship of rule and submission in marriage had to be secured by the power of the law. De Tocqueville's formulation of sexual difference relies on a different strategy. It claims the complementarity of male and female nature and the incommensurate qualities of women's separate rights and obligations. The harsh edges of domination are thus softened by a rhetoric that celebrates women's unique mission as guardians and nurturers of the conditions of citizenship. As we have seen, however, de Tocqueville's text speaks two languages, and they do not always operate in harmony. His argument oscillates between the elevated place of women in the political culture of modern democracy, on the one hand, and the need to surround their assigned space by the coercive sanctions of the marriage law, on the other.

Citizenship without gender boundaries?

The understanding of inequality as beneficial complementarity and the special moral and cultural connotations that pertain to the traditional order of marriage are still of relevance today. True, the law of marriage has in the past hundred years undergone significant changes. The enforced inequality of status between husband and wife has in Western societies largely disappeared. A married woman now can lay claim to most of the formal qualifications and benefits of citizenship. Her citizen rights are no longer mediated through the status of a wife; they belong to her as an individual. Yet, the pathetically low level of representation in virtually all forums of political decision-making leaves no doubt that women are still second-class citizens. Marriage and family, as we know them today, still trap them in a vicious 'cycle of socially caused and distinctly asymmetrical vulnerability'.[19] The asymmetry begins with the expectations, fostered already in childhood and adolescence, that they will be the primary carers of children and thus will have to rely on the stronger earning power of their husbands. As the premature closure of their future life chances will discourage young women from making use of educational and training opportunities that would fully develop their abilities, it will subsequently lead them to be content with unsatisfactory and lower paid positions in the world of work. Such structural disadvantages tend to be reinforced by the actual division of labour in the family and by the low esteem which is generally accorded to the tasks and responsibilities within the private sphere of the household. The cycle may close in conditions of poverty in old age for all those women whose entitlement to pension benefits takes no account of the years spent on raising children. The worst effects of the unequal distribution of resources and power within marriage become apparent in the consequences of divorce and in the deprivations which it frequently inflicts on wives and their children.[20]

We can say that 'vulnerability by marriage' is still the strongest among the many barriers that hold back women's claim to equal citizenship. How can this cycle be broken? What, in other words, can dispel the long shadow cast by the history of dominance and subordination? Simply to claim the gender-neutral constitution of citizenship as the end point in a by now completed process of legal and political emancipation is to trivialize the nature of the task. Its purpose cannot be to chart the successful transition from a state of exclusion to one of inclusion precisely because these two states have in the past been inseparably connected. The exercise of 'including' women in the ready-made, gender-neutral spaces of traditional conceptions of citizenship would be futile. There are no such spaces. The question is rather whether contemporary political theory contains the moral and conceptual resources for redesigning the relationship between marriage and citizenship in a way that would free both from the divisions of gender.

Among feminist political theorists there is profound disagreement about the starting point from which such reconstruction should be undertaken. Does it involve a radical break with the past, i.e. the abandonment of any universalist language of citizenship? Or, is it possible to develop genuinely human meanings of citizenship by turning the egalitarian potential of liberal political philosophy against its gender-biased conclusions?

If, as some writers have argued, not only the idea of the citizen but even that of the 'individual' – the abstract figure of the moral agent and rights bearer – has always been built upon the assumption of men's dominance, then we cannot presume the capacity of such concepts to express the moral and political agency of women. It would be no less illusory to expect that the structure of marriage could be changed in the direction of genuinely contractual equality, if not only the flawed status-contract of marriage but the very notion of contractual freedom and obligation have in the past partaken in the legitimation of 'civil slavery'.[21] In a thus radically transformed landscape of our philosophical traditions, from which the familiar contours of universalist principles have disappeared, we can find no orientation for rethinking the conditions of women's citizenship. Political theory would have to start afresh from the premise of women's difference and particular identity. That does not necessarily imply that we need to fall back upon the kind of biological essentialism which in the past has served as the linchpin of women's alleged incapacity for citizen status. Difference as the constitutive attribute of women's identity might be understood as the cumulative effect of their history of oppression. From this starting point, women's citizenship, like that of other oppressed groups, would have to align itself with the idea of a civic public built upon the recognition of heterogeneity and plurality.[22] How exactly an institutional system derived from the postulate of group difference would work, and what place or function it would attribute to marriage can, at this point in time, not be mapped out in detail. Answers to such questions would evolve from praxis, from the self-organization of women and from the dialogue between autonomous groups.

Other writers, most notably Susan Moller Okin in *Justice, Gender, and the Family*, have cashed in on the egalitarian commitments of liberal political philosophy. Okin makes use of the Rawlsian principles of justice to reflect on the institutional arrangements of a society that would include women and men, as persons, in the idea of common citizenship. Okin changes the perspectives of Rawls' original situation of justice by adding a person's sex to those particularities which are hidden from the participants by the veil of ignorance, that is, which are to be considered irrelevant to considerations of justice. It is an obvious proviso, yet it significantly transforms the procedures and the outcome of the arguments about social justice. That it is absent in Rawls' arguments, as in those of most of his critics, demonstrates once again how little attention political theory today still gives to a central terrain of social life in which the conditions of citizenship are created and transmitted to future generations.

The core institution of a society freed from the divisions of gender would be the genderless marriage. It would be an association within which the distribution of both material advantages and of more intangible goods, like independence, mutual respect and the resources for active participation in politics, would no longer follow the boundaries of sexual difference. The changes necessary to bring about such a state of affairs would, no doubt, be vast. But they are not unimaginable. At the very basic level of present inequality, society would have to guarantee that physical violence in marriage could no longer shelter behind the indifference of the law. Public policies aimed at employment, taxation, provision of child care would enable men and women to share paid and unpaid (domestic) work, productive and reproductive labour and thus to overcome what today is the main bastion of divided citizenship. As a consequence of legal reforms towards the egalitarian marriage and family we can imagine reformed educational practices, both at home and in schools. They would ensure that children no longer learn the meanings of citizenship through the lenses of sex stereotypes.

THE CONDITION OF CITIZENSHIP

In the train of such institutional and cultural changes we could, finally, envisage that marriage will more readily become what has so often been claimed for it – a bond of companionship and friendship.

It could, of course, be objected that changes of this magnitude by far transcend the legitimate concerns and the competence of the law. This chapter has attempted to show that law cannot be understood as the repository of technical rules which affect but the formal, non-substantive dimensions of social relationships. We have seen how strongly and pervasively the legal fixation of the status of husband and wife has in the past influenced the argument about citizenship. The construction of marriage in the language of quasi-political rule (*patria potestas, imperium maritale, baron and feme*) and in the rhetoric of benevolent complementarity released powerful images which became entrenched in the understanding of women as exemplary non-citizens. There is no good reason why laws aimed at an egalitarian marriage should not work in the other direction and – positively – affect the culture of citizenship.

Notes

1 Cf. T.H. Marshall, 'Citizenship and social class', in T.H. Marshall, *Class, Citizenship and Social Development* (Greenwood Press, Westport, CT, 1976), pp. 65–122, esp. p. 76; Robert A. Dahl, *A Preface to Economic Democracy* (University of California Press, Berkeley and Los Angeles, 1985) esp. pp. 11–23; Ursula Vogel, 'Is citizenship gender-specific?', in Ursula Vogel and M. Moran (eds), *The Frontiers of Citizenship* (Macmillan, London, 1991), pp. 58–85.

2 Cf. Carole Pateman, *The Sexual Contract* (Polity Press, Cambridge, 1988), Ch 1.

3 Roger Cotterrell, *The Sociology of Law: an Introduction* (Butterworths, London, 1984), Ch. 2.

4 Cf. Ute Gerhard, 'Die Rechtsstellung der Frauen in der bürgerlichen Gesellschaft des 19. Jahrhunderts', and Ursula Vogel, 'Patriarchale Herrschaft, bürgerliches Recht, bürgerliche Utopie. Eigentumsrechte der Frauen in Deutschland und England', in Jürgen Kocka (ed.), *Bürgertum im 19. Jahrhundert* vol. 1 (Deutscher Taschenbuch, Munich, 1988), pp. 439–68 and pp. 406–38.

5 Cf. Franz Wieacker, *Privatrechtsgeschichte der Neuzeit* (Vandenhoeck & Ruprecht, Gottingen, 1967), part IV.

6 Cf. Dieter Schwab, *Grundlagen und Gestalt der Staatlichen Ehegesetzgebung in der Neuzeit bis zum Beginn des 19. Jahrhunderts* (Bielefeld, 1967); Manfred Erle, *Die Ehe im Naturrecht des 17. Jahrhunderts.* (Diss, Göttingen, 1952); Alfred Dufour, *Le marriage dans l'école Allemande du droit naturel* (Librairie Générale de Droit et de Jurisprudence, Paris, 1971); Stefan Buchholz, *Recht, Religion und Ehe* (Frankfurt am Main, 1988).

7 Samuel Pufendorf, *Acht Bücher vom Natur- und Völkerrechte* (Friedrich Knochen, Frankfurt, 1711); Christian Wolff, *Grundsatze des Natur- und Völkerrechts* (Rengerische Buchhandlung, Halle, 1754).

8 Cf. Ursula Vogel, 'Political philosophers and the trouble with polygamy: patriarchal reasoning in modern natural law', *History of Political Thought*, vol. 12(2), summer 1991, pp. 229–51.

9 Pufendorf, *Acht Bücher*, VI,I,15.

10 Ibid., VI,I,10.

11 Cf. Keith Thomas, 'The double standard', *Journal of the History of Ideas*, 20 (1959), pp. 195–216; Ursula Vogel, 'Whose property? The double standard of adultery in nineteenth century law', in Carol Smart (ed.), *Regulating Womanhood: Historical Essays on Marriage, Motherhood and Sexuality* (Routledge, London, 1992), pp. 147–65.

12 Cf. Alexis de Tocqueville, *Democracy in America* (Collins, London and Glasgow, 1968 edn), pp. 763–81.

13 Ibid., p. 778.

14 Ibid., p. 777.

15 Ibid., p. 766.

16 Ibid., p. 761.

17 Ibid., p. 766.

18 Cf. Nancy Rosenblum, *Another Liberalism. Romanticism and the Reconstruction of Liberal Thought* (Harvard University Press, Cambridge, MA, 1987).

19 Susan Okin, *Justice, Gender and the Family* (Basic Books, New York, 1989), p. 138.

20 Cf. ibid., ch. 7.

21 Pateman, *The Sexual Contract*, ch. 2.

22 Cf. Iris M. Young, 'Impartiality and the civic public', in Seyla Benhabib and D. Cornell (eds), *Feminism as Critique* (Polity Press, Cambridge, 1987), pp. 56–76 and Iris M. Young, 'Polity and group difference: a critique of the idea of universal citizenship', in Cass R. Suustein (ed.), Feminism and Political Theory (University of Chicago Press, Chicago and London, 1990), pp. 117–42.

8

CIVIL CITIZENSHIP AGAINST SOCIAL CITIZENSHIP? ON THE IDEOLOGY OF CONTRACT-VERSUS-CHARITY

Nancy Fraser and Linda Gordon

'Citizen' and 'citizenship' are powerful words. They speak of respect, of rights, of dignity. Consider the meaning and emotion packed into the French *citoyen* of 1789, a word that condemned tyranny and social hierarchy, while affirming self-government and status equality; that was a moment when even women succeeded in claiming address as *citoyenne* rather than as *madame* or *mademoiselle*. Since then the word appears often as a prefix to another term, always adding dignity to the original, as in 'citizen-soldier', 'citizen-worker', 'citizen-mother'. The word has so much dignity it rarely appears in slang. In a few informal phrases it continues to carry approval and respect, as in 'a citizen of the world' or a 'citizens' committee'. We find no pejorative uses. It is a weighty, monumental, humanist word.

It is telling, therefore, that Americans rarely speak of 'social citizenship'. That expression, if used, would convey the idea that in a welfare state citizenship carries entitlements to social provision. It would bring social provision within the aura of dignity surrounding 'citizenship' and 'rights'. People who enjoy 'social citizenship' get 'social rights', not 'handouts'. This means not only that they enjoy guarantees of help in forms that maintain their status as full members of society entitled to 'equal respect'. It also means that they share a common set of institutions and services designed for all citizens, the use of which constitutes the practice of social citizenship: for example, public schools, public parks, universal social insurance, public health services. Thus, the expression 'social citizenship' evokes themes from three major traditions of political theory: liberal themes of (social) rights and equal respect; communitarian norms of solidarity and shared responsibility; and republican ideals of participation in public life (through use of 'public goods' and 'public services').

But the expression 'social citizenship' is almost never heard in public debate in the United States today. Here, social provision remains largely outside the aura of dignity surrounding 'citizenship'. Receipt of 'welfare' is usually considered grounds for disrespect, a threat to, rather than a realization of, citizenship. And in the area of social services, the word 'public' is often pejorative. Public hospitals are institutions of last resort, sites not of solidarity but of stigma. Public schools, once considered 'cradles of citizenship', are often so inferior to their 'private' (commodified) counterparts as to fit the larger pattern of 'private wealth, public squalor'. And public parks are often too dangerous to enter. In general, the idea of social citizenship in a welfare state is out of phase with powerful currents in contemporary American political culture. The connotations of citizenship are so positive, powerful and proud, while those of 'welfare' are so negative, weak and degraded, that 'social citizenship' here sounds almost oxymoronic.

If 'social citizenship' designates an absence in US political discourse, civil citizenship is emphatically a presence. Americans pride themselves on a commitment to civil liberties and civil rights, even when they do not always respect them in practice. Phrases like 'individual liberties' and 'freedom of speech' are central to the country's rhetorical traditions, despite frequent efforts to curtail them. So resonant and powerful are these themes that collective movements have sometimes sought to harness their prestige to social egalitarian aims – witness the 'civil rights movement' for racial equality.

US political culture thus combines a richly elaborated discourse of 'civil citizenship' with a near-total absence of discourse about 'social citizenship'. Consequently, American thinking about social provision has been shaped largely by images drawn from civil citizenship, especially images of contract. The result is a cultural tendency to focus on two, rather extreme, forms of human relationship: discrete contractual exchanges of equivalents, on the one hand, and unreciprocated, unilateral charity, on the other. Most debates over welfare-state policy have been framed in terms of this contract-versus-charity opposition. Invidious distinctions are drawn between 'contributory' programmes and 'non-contributory' ones, between social insurance – where beneficiaries have a right to what they receive since they merely 'get back what they put in', and public assistance – where they have no such right since they 'get something for nothing'. 'Social citizenship', in contrast, points to another sort of relationship altogether. Its absence in the public discourse of the United States betokens – and strengthens – a cultural suppression of alternatives to the stark binary opposition, contract versus charity.

For these reasons, the expression 'social citizenship' provides some leverage for understanding, and criticizing, American political culture. It is not, however, without difficulties of its own. Not only does it presuppose the increasingly problematic unit of the nation-state – a *major* difficulty we shall not discuss here – but standard conceptions of social citizenship are pervaded by androcentrism and ethnocentrism. In what follows, then, we proceed simultaneously on two fronts. We use a concept derived largely from English sociological theory to critique American political culture, while at the same time, we use aspects of American history and culture to reveal some limitations of the English concept.

The legacy of T.H. Marshall

Our touchstone is T.H. Marshall's brilliant 1949 essay, 'Citizenship and social class', the source for all discussions of 'social citizenship'. Marshall was the first to conceptualize and defend social citizenship as the crowning stage in the historical development of modern citizenship. In his conception, it was the last of three stages. The first stage, *civil citizenship*, he held to have been constructed primarily in the eighteenth century and to have established the rights necessary for individual freedom: rights to property and personal liberty, and especially the right to justice. The second stage, *political citizenship*, was built primarily in the nineteenth century, in his view, and encompassed the right to participate in the exercise of political power, whether by holding office or by voting. The third and final stage, *social citizenship*, was constructed in the twentieth century; in Marshall's view, it not only encompassed rights to a modicum of economic security, but also entailed a more far-reaching right 'to a share in the full social heritage and to live the life of a civilized being according to the standards prevailing in the society'.[1]

Marshall wrote, of course, at a moment of hopefulness about social citizenship. The British electorate after the Second World War 'ungratefully' overthrew Churchill and installed a Labour government committed to building a welfare state. Marshall envisaged a state that would not only smooth the roughest edges off the sharp inequalities of class society, but actually erode some class-based status differences altogether. He wrote of the importance of universal provision in creating status equality and social solidarity:

> Even when benefits are paid in cash . . . class fusion is outwardly expressed in the form of a new common experience. All learn what it means to have an insurance card . . . or to collect children's allowances or pensions from the post office. But where the benefit takes the form of a service, the qualitative element [of shared experience and common status] enters into the benefit itself, and not only into the process by which it is obtained. The extension of such services can therefore have a profound effect on the qualitative aspects of social differentiation.[2]

Marshall envisioned that universal education and health services would eventually help dissolve divergent class cultures into a 'unified civilization' by progressively decoupling real income from money income. He anticipated that the 'minimum standard' established by public provision would in time be raised so high as to approach the maximum, so that the extras the rich could buy would be mere frills. The public service, not the purchased service, would become the norm.

Marshall's utopianism did not derive from a simple Whiggish view of progress. On the contrary, he analysed contradictions among the three evolving dimensions of citizenship as well as tensions among the citizens. He noted those excluded from citizenship and understood that citizenship itself had functioned as an architect of social inequality. He also grappled with the question of whether a uniform status of citizenship could be achieved while respecting the inviolability of market mechanisms and private property. He concluded, however, that the further development of social citizenship could renovate social relations towards greater equality.

T.H. Marshall's essay is tonic reading in this period of widespread pessimism about public life, but it should not be appropriated uncritically. When questions about gender and race are put at the centre of the enquiry, key elements of Marshall's analysis become problematic. His periodization of the three stages of citizenship, for example, fits the experience of white working men only, a minority of the population. His conceptual distinctions between civil, political and social citizenship presuppose, rather than problematize, gender and racial hierarchy. Finally, his assumption, continued in later social-democratic thought and practice, that the chief aim of social citizenship is erosion of *class* inequality and protection from *market* forces slights other key axes of inequality and other mechanisms and arenas of domination.

Most important for our purposes here, however, is Marshall's optimism about the ease with which social citizenship could be built upon a foundation laid in terms of civil citizenship. This optimism seems misplaced from the standpoint of the contemporary United States, where we find not only new depths of immiseration and inequality, but also new levels of conservative hostility to a welfare state. This hostility is often expressed in terms of the contractual norms of civil citizenship – in the idea that welfare recipients are getting something for nothing, that they are violating standards of equal exchange. Such formulations prompt us to consider whether the cultural mythology of civil citizenship may not stunt the capacity to envision social citizenship.

In what follows, we re-examine the relationship between civil citizenship and social citizenship. (We leave aside questions about the relationship between political citizenship and social citizenship, although they, too, would repay re-examination in the light of gender and race.) Our focus is the historical construction of the opposition between contract and charity. We trace the genealogy of this opposition from its origins in the cultural mythology of contract surrounding civil citizenship to its current role in stunting the development of social citizenship in the United States. In so doing, we take special care to reveal the important but neglected role of gender and race in structuring these cultural conceptions.

Commercial myths/civil wrongs

The first 'stage' of citizenship in Marshall's analysis – civil citizenship – by no means spelled progress for all affected. Rather, in raising the status of some it simultaneously lowered the relative status of others, since the understandings that informed civil citizenship helped construct modern forms of male dominance and white supremacy, as well as of class exploitation. Nor can the development of civil citizenship be understood in isolation from the question of entitlements to social provision. All societies contain people who cannot obtain their subsistence in the socially normative way, people who are disabled or who lack family help, for example. The new individual property rights that emerged with civil citizenship frequently undercut the traditional claims of such persons for community support. The result was a gendered, ideological opposition between contract and charity that still structures state provision of welfare today.[3]

Let us not be misunderstood. We do not claim that civil rights are inherently antithetical to social rights. Current ideological antitheses between entitlement and charity are constructed and contingent, not conceptually necessary. The civil rights of citizenship need not be cloaked in commercial metaphors of contractual exchange. Re-imagining these rights in better, more solidaristic ways remains a crucial task for political theorists and social movements. What follows is a critical prelude to such re-imagination.

The earliest English meaning of 'citizenship' was residence in a city. Since city dwellers were among the first groups to free themselves from feudal relations of servitude, the term also carried connotations of freedom. Marshall placed the beginnings of modern citizenship in early modern England, where by the eighteenth century permanent and hereditary servility had been legally abolished. 'Citizenship' at this time meant free status, and the rights attaching to that status were called 'civic' or 'civil rights'. These included the right to own property and to make valid contracts, the right to sue in court, the liberty of one's person and, after the English Revolution, freedom of speech, thought and religious faith.

Thus, civil citizenship brought important new 'civil' rights to many people. These rights did not arrive in the form of thin, abstract moral norms, however, but came laden with cultural meanings and images. Liberal social-contract theory supplied many of the cultural trappings. It justified modern constitutional government by tracing the origin of legitimate political power to a voluntary, conventional agreement among free, rational 'men' in 'the state of nature'. The result of their 'original pact' was government by law and, simultaneously, its other face: the legal constitution of a 'civil' sphere within society in which independent individuals could contract freely with one another, secure in their persons and in their property. These individuals thus acquired legal personalities and civil rights; they became 'citizens' of 'civil society'.

The constitution of 'civil society', both in contract theory and in contract law, was tantamount to a revolution in social ontology. The subjects of civil society were 'individuals', conceived as prior to their relationships. Relationships, in turn, were cast as voluntary, temporary and limited arrangements entered into out of individual self-interest. The prototype was the contractual agreement, which consisted of an exchange of equivalents. This presupposed the liberty and independence of the contractors, neutral mechanisms to enforce their agreements, and individual property in the items exchanged, be they commodities, labour power or opinions. In C.B. Macpherson's memorable phrase, civil society was premised on a 'possessive individualism'.[4]

'Possessive individualism' was prototypically the basis of economic exchange, but its conceptual reach was far wider. It underlay the whole of modern civil society, itself broader than, albeit modelled on, commerce. The ability to enter freely into agreements or relationships of any kind presupposed freedom from subjection to a master, a condition that was imaged as self-ownership. 'Individuals', therefore, were proprietors not only of tangible goods in their possession but of their 'persons' as well. The guarantees of civil citizenship thus included not just economic property rights, including the right to sell one's labour power, but also rights to personal liberty – freedom from arbitrary imprisonment and from unreasonable search and seizure; liberty of movement and bodily integrity; freedom of speech, thought, and religion – and the right to sue in a court of law in order to enforce all one's other rights.

Certainly, this property-centred contract model is not the only way of conceiving civil society. In the eighteenth and nineteenth centuries, another model, less economistic, more 'associational' was developed by Montesquieu and de Tocqueville, among others, but the contract model has predominated in the United States, supplying the images and interpretations that have coloured understanding of civil citizenship.

Commonsensical as it is today, the new ontology of civil society represented a revolutionary departure from earlier views of personhood and social relations. Previous legal understandings did not recognize 'individuals' as bearing rights that were prior to, and independent of, their place in a status hierarchy. Nor did they construe social relations as freely chosen, limited agreements between parties of equal status. Rather, relationally defined statuses were cast as prior to or contemporary with individuals and constitutive of their entitlements and obligations. Relationships, moveover, were characteristically quasi-permanent, non-voluntary, hierarchical arrangements obligating subordinates to obey and superordinates to protect. This earlier ontology recognized masters and subjects but had no place for citizens.

The contract-centred construction of civil citizenship presented a fundamental challenge to traditional subjectship but was not meant to replace it wholesale. Not even the most radical early exponents of 'civil society' envisioned it as the whole of society, nor did they see all human beings as 'individuals'. Women, of course, were excluded from independent civil (and political) citizenship for centuries, and there was no agreement on what degree of citizenship should be accorded the poor, servile and 'racially different'. Consequently, civil society was viewed as but one subsector within society, standing in a complex, symbiotic relation to others.

Coverture and slavery

We can exemplify the apparent paradoxes here by considering two modern forms of subjection, coverture and slavery. In the legal fiction of coverture, married women were subsumed into the legal personalities of their husbands. This looks at first like a continuation of traditional subjectship, which is how T.H. Marshall apparently saw it. But coverture is better understood as a modern phenomenon that helped *constitute* civil citizenship. Coverture was a stage in the decline of patriarchy. (By patriarchy we mean not just relations between men and women but societies pervaded by hierarchical relations, in which nearly everyone was subordinate to some superior, whether king, lord, landlord, father or husband.)

With the construction of modern civil society, however, married men who would have earlier been 'dependents' within larger patriarchal units became family 'heads' and 'individuals'. Family headship thus became a newly salient and honorific status, rivalling rank, caste and property ownership as a source of civil citizenship. By granting independent legal standing to all (white) male heads of families, coverture democratized relations and undercut patriarchy among adult free (that is, in the US, white) men, for whom marriage conferred 'independence' and full civil, if not yet electoral, rights. *Contra* Marshall's assumption, then, the exclusion of married women from civil citizenship was no mere archaic vestige destined to fade as citizenship evolved. Rather, women's subsumption in coverture was the other face and enabling ground of modern civil citizenship. The two mutually defined one another.

The same is true for the brutal new forms of slavery that emerged in the New World in tandem with the elaboration of civil citizenship. In the United States, for example, the world's most extensive civil rights for white men coexisted with history's most totalitarian, rights-depriving system of chattel slavery for black men and women. The modern 'scientific' concept of 'race' justified the subjection of blacks at the very moment when the discourse of 'citizenship' proclaimed liberty the natural birthright of 'man'. The centrepiece of civil citizenship in 'the white republic' was a property conception of rights. In the slave states, free white men were 'persons', while black slaves were 'property', and civil citizenship guaranteed the property rights of the former in the latter. In one of the great ironies in the history of civil citizenship, the first United States Married Women's Property Act, passed in Mississippi in 1839, was aimed at securing slaveholders' wives rights over slaves.[5] Meanwhile, the citizenship claims of white male wage workers rested in part on their ability to claim their labour power as a form of personal property.

'Free labour' found its meaning and honour largely in contrast to the degraded condition of the slave, who laboured but did not earn.[6] Here, too, then, arrangements treated by Marshall as peripheral exceptions helped construct core cultural meanings of civil citizenship.

Civil citizenship made property rights the model for all other rights, thereby encouraging people to translate all sorts of claims into property claims. It is not surprising, then, that those excluded from civil citizenship were usually those who did not own property, either because they were unable to get their resources defined as property (for example women, tenants), or because they *were* property (slaves). Similarly, some civil rights functioned to the disadvantage of the propertyless. Rights accorded to heads of households against intruders and the state, for example, often deprived slaves, women, workers and children of outside protection to stop abuse by their masters.[7]

Notwithstanding the rhetoric of liberal contract theory, then, civil rights were not at first rights of 'individuals'. They belonged, instead to white male property owners and family heads, often by virtue of their responsibility for 'dependents'. 'Having dependents', in fact, became in some jurisdictions a qualification for full civil citizenship. The legal subsumption of wives in coverture, and the legal classification of slaves as property, therefore, were no simple matters of exclusion. They actually helped instead to define civil citizenship, for it was by protecting, subsuming and even owning others that white male property owners and family heads became citizens.

Marshall was not quite right, then, in viewing the construction of civil citizenship as simply an elevation in the status of those men whom it freed from the bonds of dependency. It also represented a comparative demotion in status for those women, men and children who did not then acquire independent legal personalities. Previously, to lack civil 'independence' had been the normal majority condition; it was not particularly stigmatized or demeaning. But when white married men, small freeholders, and family heads achieved independent legal status, subsumption into the legal personality of another became increasingly anomalous – and stigmatizing. By the mid-nineteenth century, both coverture and slavery had come to seem abhorrent to many people. Some white women and black slaves responded by appropriating the rhetoric of social contract theory and claiming to be 'individuals'. But, in so doing, they were not simply demanding admission to a pre-existing status. Rather, they were challenging the grounds on which claims to social resources were made, a fundamental aspect of the social order.

The erosion of communal responsibility

The construction of modern civil citizenship also transformed the basis of entitlements to social resources, which had implications for 'social welfare'. In traditional, precapitalist societies, claims to resources were often grounded in some variation of a 'moral economy' that curbed individual self-interest. Ownership was usually a matter of divided, overlapping entitlements to various kinds of use. As a result, most property was not entirely liquid, its disposition being constrained by tradition. Moral-economic understandings also constrained the conditions surrounding paid labour, removing it too from 'free' market exchange. The remuneration, the content of the labour, who performed it and when – all were hedged in by a tradition that constrained all parties to the transaction.

In this context, claims on social resources were based on a variety of relationships, and many entitlements to support derived from kinship. The traditional extended family gave a wide range of kinfolk, and at times neighbours and villagers, had some economic responsibilities for each other. No single relationship defined anyone's whole entitlement to support; every particular relationship formed a link in a longer chain of dependence. These arrangements were patriarchal, to be sure, but they differed markedly from coverture. Women figured as centrally as men, though without as much power, in the full range of community and kin-based relationships. Instead of depending exclusively on husbands, wives usually had a variety of different bases on which to claim needed resources.

The rise of civil citizenship eroded these arrangements, in part by creating a new form of property right that trumped customary obligations and entitlements. When land became a commodity, rural populations lost their customary rights of tenancy and use. Later, 'reforms' of traditional poor relief weakened established patterns of community support, facilitating the creation of a 'free' market in labour – free, that is, from the moral-economic strictures of the 'just wage'. For the majority, consequently, the property right enshrined by civil citizenship spelled dispossession.

It was just such new forms of property right and labour contract that T.H. Marshall had in mind when he claimed that the rise of civil citizenship at first set back social citizenship, impacting negatively on the welfare of many. But he failed to notice the gender and family meanings of civil citizenship, which helped create the norm of the family wage and undercut earlier, kin-based claims on social resources.[8]

Kinship and contract

These arrangements signalled the contraction of kinship to one 'sphere' of society, a counterpoint to, and support for, 'civil society'. Whereas all social relations had earlier been formed from or modelled on kinship, kinship now became merely one social arena among others, and its cultural meaning altered.[9] From the eighteenth century, the 'kinship sphere' became hegemonically defined as the realm of 'the feminine' and 'the domestic', a 'private sphere' of familial intimacy and affect. The result was the appearance, especially among the urban bourgeoisie and those who aspired to middle class status, of a new ideological disjuncture between two different kinds of claims to social resources, associated with two different spheres of society. In civil society, the 'male sphere', contractual relations dominated: resources were exchanged for exact equivalents in discrete, monetarized transactions between self-interested independent individuals. In the domestic sphere of the intimate family, in contrast, resources appeared to flow with sentiment wholly outside the circuit of exchange.

This gender division between the two spheres was ideological in several respects. The norms it propounded were constantly violated in practice, and different social groups sought to refashion them to serve different political agendas. For example, working-class men and women used ideas of womanly 'domesticity' in their struggles for better living and working conditions and to develop their own working-class notions of discipline and respectability. Likewise, women's rights activists used domesticity ideas to argue for the importance of women's influence as mothers.

The 'male' side of the divide, contractual exchange, was increasingly represented as the basic form of human interaction. Contract became a metaphor for the presupposition of rational choice in which the motive was self-advantage. It was applied even to non-market spheres, such as politics, as well as to commercial relations. Within commerce, moreover, the contract metaphor reconstructed the meaning of paid labour as 'wage labour', a supposedly free and equal contractual exchange of labour power for wages. This extension of the contract model redounded back in turn upon representations of the 'female sphere', making kinship and intimate relations appear to be 'natural', hence outside the province of social theory.

As contract gained ascendance over a progressively larger share of human relations, the range of alternatives seemed to narrow. Non-contractual forms of reciprocity were increasingly assimilated to contractual exchange, except for those 'inside' the nuclear family. Any interactions that seemed neither contractual nor familial now appeared to be unilateral and entirely voluntary, entailing neither entitlements nor responsibilities. Thus, the hegemony of contract helped to generate a specifically modern conception of 'charity' as its complementary other. In this conception, charity appeared as a pure, unilateral gift, on which the recipient had no claim and for which the donor had no obligation. Thus, whereas contract connoted equal exchange, mutual benefit, self-interest, rationality and masculinity, charity took on contrasting connotations of inequality, unilateral gift-giving, altruism, sentiment, and, at times, femininity. The contrast, moreover, assumed the guise of a stable, conceptually exhaustive dichotomy: all extra-familial relations had to be either contractual or charitable. There appeared to be no other possibilities.

The binary opposition between contract and charity had still further ideological consequences. First, in the modern conception of charity, the giver got moral credit while the taker was increasingly stigmatized. That distribution of value was inherently unstable, however, since the stigmatization of recipients naturally spawned doubts about the merits of giving. From at least the nineteenth century, such doubts fuelled repeated waves of 'reform' that sought to counter the 'degenerative' effects of 'indiscriminate giving' both on recipients and on society as a whole. Thus the contract side of the opposition repeatedly menaced the charity side, and what had appeared to be a stable dichotomy was always in danger of dissolving.

Secondly, because the contract/charity dichotomy shrouded the very possibility of non-contractual reciprocity, it rendered invisible a whole range of popular practices that defied the official binary categorization. Kinship, neighbourly and community obligations continued to be strong, despite the ideology of the independent nuclear family; and informal mutual aid persisted in a variety of guises and forms. Yet these practices lost public recognition and official political legitimacy. In time, the lack of a language to validate their existence contributed to their decline and decay. Throughout the nineteenth century, moreover, while charity was under constant attack, the definition of kinship was becoming more nuclear. Economic responsibilities for extended family members were growing weaker in the United States, thus further constricting the experience of interpersonal help that was neither contractual nor charitable.

Contract, charity and welfare

The contract-versus-charity dichotomy thus to some extent remade reality in its image, crowding out other types of relations. It impressed its stamp strongly on state provision of welfare, which developed along dichotomous lines. In the United States, government programmes from early in the twentieth century divided into two streams. Those with the most legitimacy took on some of the trappings of civil exchange, guaranteeing secure entitlements to some citizens by mimicking private contracts. Other programmes, in contrast, were cast as proffering unreciprocated aid to the 'innocent' and 'deserving' poor, with the state assuming the role of previously private charity. These two streams, moreover, were strongly gendered. The contract stream had its first US prototype in 'workman's compensation' (industrial accident insurance), while the charity stream was exemplified by 'widows' pensions'.[10]

The gender-coded contract-versus-charity dichotomy persists today in many countries in the opposition between 'social insurance' and 'public assistance' programmes. The first were designed by reformers to appear 'contributory', seemingly embodying the principle of exchange; recipients, originally intended to be male and relatively privileged members of the working class, are defined as 'entitled'.[11] 'Public assistance', in contrast, continued the 'non-contributory' charity tradition, so that its recipients appear to get something for nothing, in violation of contractual norms.

That, at least, is the official appearance, but the reality is considerably more complicated. Numerous social insurance advocates of the early twentieth century knowingly used the term 'contributory' as a rhetorical selling device for the new programmes, fully aware that all welfare programmes are financed through contributions, differing only as to where and how these are collected, through sales taxes, wage deductions, etc. Despite their official image as contractual, US social security 'insurance' programmes depart significantly from actuarial principles, and benefits do not actually reflect financial contributions. And while the legitimacy of social security retirement pensions derives in part from the view that they compensate previous service, one might with equal plausibility claim that seemingly 'non-contributory' programmes like Aid to Families with Dependent Children (AFDC, the successor to mother's pensions) compensate the child-rearing 'service' of single mothers.[12] In any case, the contract-versus-charity dichotomy is less a true picture of the two tiers of American state provision than an ideology of their differential legitimacy. But that differential ultimately rests on the privileging of waged labour and on the derogation of women's unpaid care work.[13]

As the cultural mythology of civil citizenship affected the design of welfare programmes, so too has the stratified, gendered construction of social welfare shaped the terms of civil citizenship. Receipt of public assistance has often carried curtailment of civil rights. For example, AFDC claimants in the United States have been denied the right to interstate travel (abridged by state residency requirements); the right to due process (abridged by administrative procedures for determining eligibility and terminating benefits); the right to protection from unreasonable search and seizure (abridged by unannounced home visits); the right to privacy (abridged by 'morals testing'); and the right to equal protection (abridged by all of the above). In the 1960s and 1970s United States courts overturned many of these practices, but the 1970s and 1980s brought a rash of new restrictions. By contrast, receipt of 'social insurance' entailed no comparable loss of civil rights.

Significantly, in the 1960s and 1970s, legal arguments aimed at securing recipients' civil rights sought to establish that welfare benefits are not a 'gratuity' or 'promise of charity' but a form of 'property'. Inspired by the 'new property' theory of Charles Reich,[14] these arguments were designed to conform to the reigning interpretation of the due process clause of the US Constitution. This clause guarantees procedural protections against deprivations of life, liberty and property, but claims couched as protections of property have proved most successful in practice. Welfare-rights lawyers calculated that their best chance lay in arguing that claimants had property rights in welfare and were therefore entitled to a hearing before denial or termination of benefits. There was no legal precedent, in contrast, for the simpler and more straightforward argument that denying means of subsistence to the poor violated their constitutional rights to life and liberty.[15]

In this interpretation and the surrounding arguments, the contract-versus-charity dichotomy is clear. Only by reclassifying public assistance as property and recasting recipients as independent contractors could their civil citizenship be maintained. Yet as some welfare rights activists noted at the time, these terms could not express a vision of full social citizenship. The arguments from welfare as property yielded some procedural safeguards, but they did not establish a substantive right to economic security in the form of an adequate grant. Although public assistance recipients won right to a hearing, they won no right to be lifted out of poverty, let alone any right 'to a share in the full social heritage and to live the life of a civilized being according to the standards prevailing in the society'.[16]

In the contract-versus-charity dichotomy, contract is the more powerful pole. It is understandable, therefore, that reformers seeking to win social rights tried to move 'welfare' from the charity to the property side of the line. They bent the property idiom to new purposes, but they ran up against the limits of a strategy that sought to model social provision after a contract-centred model of civil citizenship. That strategy was necessarily fraught with tensions, since the contract-centred model of civil citizenship is premised on either/or oppositions between gift and exchange, dependence and independence, while social citizenship points beyond these oppositions to solidarity and interdependence.

More in line with the deep logic of these ideological oppositions is the recent attempt by US neo-conservatives to assimilate 'welfare' to 'contract'. Their strategy is announced in Lawrence Mead's influential book, *Beyond Entitlement: The Social Obligations of Citizenship*, which argues that citizenship is a two-sided status conferring not only rights but responsibilities.[17] Mead proposes to correct liberals' putative one-sided emphasis on welfare rights by introducing contracts in which welfare claimants must 'agree' to accept work, training and/or other obligations in return for their grants, thereby entering the sphere of exchange. Yet he neglects to explain how the proposed transaction could be a valid contract – a voluntary, free agreement between independent individuals – when one party lacks the barest means of subsistence, while the other is the US government.

The appeal of arguments like Mead's shows that the contract norm continues to hamper attempts to expand social provision today. Since the wage appears as an exchange in return for labour, it is argued that all resources should be apportioned in terms of exchange. The widespread fear that 'welfare' recipients are 'getting something for nothing' is an understandably embittered response from those who work hard and get little; their own paltry remuneration becomes their norm and they see themselves as cheated by welfare clients rather than by their employers. Such responses are of course exacerbated when the poor are represented as female, sexually immoral and/or racially 'other'. The result is that, under the impact of economic recession, the claims of the poor in the United States today are being weakened by a resurgence of the rhetoric of contract.

In sum, the cultural mythology of civil citizenship stands in a tense, often obstructing relationship to social citizenship. This is nowhere more true than in the United States, where the dominant understanding of civil citizenship remains strongly inflected by notions of 'contract' and 'independence', while social provision has been constructed to connote 'charity' and 'dependence'. What is missing is a public language capable of expressing ideas that escape those dichotomous oppositions: especially the ideas of solidarity, non-contractual reciprocity, and interdependence that are central to any humane social citizenship.

A new rhetoric of citizenship

Our analysis reveals considerable tension between the cultural mythology of civil citizenship and T.H. Marshall's conception of social citizenship. The chief obstacles to social citizenship in the United States are, of course, political and economic – international as well as domestic. Nevertheless, ideological conceptions, such as contract, make it more difficult to develop public support for a welfare state, especially where the cultural mythology of civil citizenship is highly developed. Marshall underestimated these ideological difficulties.

Should we conclude, then, that civil and social citizenship are incompatible with one another? Our analysis does not support that conclusion. On the contrary, we maintain that reconciliation of the two forms of citizenship represents an urgent task for theorists.

What would it take to revivify social citizenship in the face of the new contractarianism? One beginning is to re-imagine civil citizenship in a less property-centred, more solidaristic form. This would permit us to reclaim some of the moral and conceptual ground for social rights that has been colonized by property and contract. We might try to reconceive personal liberties in terms that nurture rather than choke-off social solidarity. Certainly we need to contest claims that the preservation of civil and political rights requires jettisoning rights to social support. Today, when rhetoric about the 'triumph of democracy' accompanies economic devastation, it is time to insist there can be no democratic citizenship without social rights.

Notes

1 T.H. Marshall, 'Citizenship and social class' in Seymour Martin Lipset (ed.), *Class, Citizenship, and Social Development: Essays by T.H. Marshall* (University of Chicago Press, Chicago, 1964), p. 78.

2 Ibid., p. 113.

3 In this chapter we use 'social citizenship' to refer to Marshall's, and others', vision of an ideal 'welfare state'; where we refer to actually existing welfare, we speak of 'social provision' or the like.

4 C.B. Macpherson, *The Political Theory of Possessive Individualism: Hobbes to Locke* (Oxford University Press, Oxford, 1974).

5 Roger M. Smith, 'One united people: second-class female citizenship and the American quest for community', *Yale Journal of Law and the Humanities*, 2, 1 (May 1989), pp. 229–93.

6 Judith Shklar *American Citizenship: the Quest for Inclusion* (Harvard University Press, Cambridge MA, 1991).

7 Some feminist theorists have concluded that privacy rights are in principle not emancipatory for women. See, for example, Catherine MacKinnon, *Feminism Unmodified* (Harvard University Press, Cambridge MA, 1989). Nevertheless, many functional rights of women originated from efforts to protect the property of their masters; this was the case, for example, of laws against (extramarital) rape.

8 That at least was the situation in theory. In fact, very few men actually earned a wage sufficient to support an economically dependent wife and children single-handedly; so the paid and unpaid labour of wives and children was crucial to the family economy. We very much need historical research to determine the precise impact of legal coverture and the individual labour market on women's kinship and community networks of sharing and provision.

9 Linda J. Nicholson, *Gender and History: the Limits of Social Theory in the Age of the Family* (Columbia University Press, New York, 1986).

10 See the essays in Linda Gordon (ed.), *Women, the State and Welfare* (University of Wisconsin Press, Wisconsin, 1991), especially the papers by Barbara J. Nelson and Diana Pearce.

11 Central to that construction, and to the entire opposition between contract and charity, is the hegemony of wage labour as the privileged basis of entitlement. This privilege is ironic, of course, since the view of the 'wage labour contract' as a free agreement between independent individuals is a mystification. Yet that friction supports the presumption that social insurance beneficiaries are independent contractors, hence full citizens of civil society.

12 Some advocates of the early twentieth-century state 'mothers' pensions' programmes, the forerunners of AFDC, justified these programmes as compensating motherhood, which they cast as a valued service to society on a par with soldiering. Yet the pensions, like AFDC later, never supported motherhood *per se* but only *single* motherhood. Moreover, the compensation-for-service view was never institutionalized and it had largely disappeared by the time the state programmes were federalized in the Social Security Act of 1935. By then wage labour had become so hegemonic that it and military service were the only bases of entitlements to provision other than abject need. See Theda Skocpol, *Protecting Mothers and Soldiers* (Harvard University Press, Cambridge MA, 1992) and Molly Ladd-Taylor, *Mother-Work* (University of Illinois Press, Champaign, 1993).

13 Moreover, there is also a third tier of provision, not even visible to the casual observer, that equally defies the dichotomy. This is the whole range of occupational 'fringe benefits' and market-purchased pensions and insurance available to unionized workers, the salaried middle classes and the wealthy. Usually considered 'private', and thus quintessentially contract as opposed to charity, this provision enjoys a tax exempt status that amounts to a major government subsidy, one that could even be considered a 'handout'. But it, too, appears legitimate because of its link to paid employment, the quintessential form of 'contribution' in a male-dominated capitalist society.

14 Charles Reich, 'The new property', *The Yale Law Journal*, 73, 5 (April 1964), pp. 733–87. Reich's article was cited in the majority opinion of the Supreme Court in *Goldberg* v. *Kelly* (1970), the decision that came closest to establishing a right to welfare.

15 For a contemporary account of the legal strategy, see Edward V. Sparer, 'The

right to welfare', in Norman Dorsen (ed.), *The Rights of Americans: What They Are – What They Should Be* (Pantheon, New York, 1970).

16 Sparer, ibid., provides the most lucid and politically astute account of the achievements and limitations of the legal strategies pursued in the late 1960s and early 1970s. For accounts of the partial erosion of procedural safeguards as a result of court decisions of the 1970s and 1980s, see Charles Reich, 'Beyond the new property: an ecological view of due process', *Brooklyn Law Review*, 56 (1990), pp. 731–45 and Sylvia Law, 'Some reflections on *Goldberg* v. *Kelly* at twenty years', *Brooklyn Law Review*, 56 (1990), pp. 805–30.

17 Lawrence Mead, *Beyond Entitlement: The Social Obligations of Citizenship* (Free Press, New York, 1986).

9

CITIZENSHIP AND CIVIL SOCIETY IN CENTRAL EUROPE

Attila Agh

The traditional role of the intelligentsia in Central Europe

All historical dramas start with the presentation of the dramatis personae, the chief actors of social life. In Western Europe these actors are the *burgher* and the *citizen*, also called *homo economicus* and *homo politicus*. Civil society and the state, with their separate but interwoven institutional structures, appear as the great fields of activity for these sectors. In Central Europe this model is well known but of no direct use. We appreciate the extensive scholarly literature about citizenship, the recent discussions around the changing features of citizens in the postmodern era and the emerging new conditions for political participation, but we cannot apply them to our situation. Our regional traditions and present processes of sociopolitical transition are so different that we have to look for other actors or, possibly, for the same actors in different guise.

In the West all members of society are supposed to be at the same time citizens and burghers. In Eastern Europe proper, these roles are virtually absent; in Central Europe both roles do exist, though they are performed by substitutes. Here, the social and political role of citizens is by tradition played by the *intelligentsia*. As a group of professional 'surrogate citizens', the intelligentsia is of crucial societal importance in Central Europe. Being the chief actors in historical changes, this group reflects or mirrors all the contradictions and ambiguities of the failed and interrupted modernizations of Central Europe. Performing as burghers as well as citizens (but mostly the first), as elites and masses (again, mostly the first, but more often also the second), as the new middle classes and the old ones (managers, professionals but also clerks and writers), the intelligentsia in this half-Westernized (and sometimes brutally Easternized) region performs Western roles in a non-Western way.

We find a composite picture of the historical and present roles of the intelligentsia in Central Europe in J. Rupnik's *The Other Europe*. From the very beginning the definition of Central Europe is intertwined with the role of the intelligentsia. The modernization process may be characterized by the fact that the gentry retained its dominant position (and turned into a political class); the bourgeoisie, on the other hand, remained small and powerless. The non-emergence of a Western-style entrepreneurial class entailed the lack of a bourgeois political elite. The state, represented by a ruling bureaucratic and political class, became the dominant instrument of modernization, actively involved in socioeconomic developments and directing the formation of social classes. Thus, 'the expanding bureaucracy flourished while civil society remained weak and fragmented, posing little challenge to the growing authority of the state'.[1]

It is important to note that, although the traditional Central European political culture reveals authoritarian predispositions, it is in general resistant to totalitarianism. The Austro-Hungarian empire was a constitutional state but not a parliamentary democracy, though it permitted limited autonomy to the civil society and to local self-government.

> The dilemma of the Central European intelligentsia . . . rested on the discrepancy between its identification with Western civilization and culture and their problematic introduction into a backward social and economic structure. The nineteenth-century intelligentsia was the 'inventor' of modern nationalism and at the same time the promotor of Western social and political ideas. Hence the origins of the intelligentsia's love affair with the state, which was thought to be the only possible guarantor of the nation's survival and the sole force capable of bringing the nation into Europe.[2]

The balance changed after the First World War with the rise of right-wing authoritarianism and national-ethnic tensions among the newly emerged nation-states. 'Though the state became semi-authoritarian, society remained ethnically, culturally and politically pluralist.'[3] After the Second World War Central European societies became ethnically, culturally and politically less and less 'pluralist'. Germans and Jews, bearers of the common German-speaking middle-class culture, had disappeared, and the nation-states strived for more ethnic and cultural homogeneity by massive expulsion of national minorities. Following this war there was a relative and short power vacuum in Central Europe. For some years the states possessed a small portion of national autonomy. In this period of national reconstruction the intelligentsia played a role, replacing parts of the old intelligentsia in a revolutionary zeal to create a new, democratic society. The imagination of the newly recruited intelligentsia was captured, at least temporarily, by the slogans of (state) socialism in the late 1940s, promising to overcome the traditional backwardness of Central European societies and thus concording with what was felt by the intelligentsia as its traditional historical mission. The role of the intelligentsia in state socialism had thus two sides to it. On the one hand, it resulted in the abandonment of the intellectuals' independence and identity; on the other hand, it was a constant fight against the overwhelming role of the state.

The Hungarian thesis

The 'Hungarian thesis' was elaborated by the Hungarian sociologists György Konrád and Iván Szelényi in *Intellectuals on the Road of Class Power* (written in 1974, published in English in 1979). This book reflects the Hungarian developments in the 1960s and 1970s (with Kadarism as the most liberal version of post-Stalinism). It expresses a general and common tendency of state socialism, stressing the central role of the rational planner or redistributor of all resources (in the terms of the authors an *étatist* mode of production). The teleology of the rationality of the planner's decisions attracts (leading) intellectuals. They become involved in the process as experts managing and perfecting the all-embracing system of pure rationalism by constant 'reforms'. The definition of the *intelligentsia* (preferred to the term 'intellectuals', emphasizing the difference between Central and Western European social structures) as a class expresses the idea of merger with apparatchiks or bureaucrats who are managing the system by concentrating and monopolizing power, but need the assistance of the (leading) intelligentsia in ruling and controlling society.

This 'Hungarian thesis' is, in some ways, an articulation of the traditional role of the intelligentsia in Central Europe and can be summarized in the following way. In the absence of a real bourgeoisie, in Central Europe it is the state which becomes the actual driving force of socioeconomic modernization. The intelligentsia identifies itself more with the state than in Western Europe, therefore both the nationalist and the socialist ideologies acquire a clearly *étatist* complexion. State socialism in this part of Europe was the culmination of a lengthy process in which the intelligentsia, as the depositories of teleological and technical knowledge, gradually merged with the modernizing state and, together with the *nomen-*

klatura and the poli-technocrats, formed a unified ruling class.[4] Against the 'Hungarian thesis' two major objections can be, and have been, raised:

1 We cannot treat the intelligentsia as a 'class', not even as a unified group; as an amalgam of heterogeneous smaller groups, having different relationships to power; it is a loosely organized major social group.
2 Other social actors should not be neglected: the former 'ruling class', exaggerating its willingness to professionalize and share its power and the newly emerging actors in the lop-sided modernization process of state socialism.

Szelényi, in a series of well-written and well-argued self-criticisms and self-defences, has never really accepted the first objection but has advanced very much along the lines of the second counter-argument. He admits that, based on the Hungarian tendencies of the 1960s and early 1970s, he has overestimated the capacity for change of the ruling bureaucracy but has returned to a modified version of his original thesis in the period of the 1989 revolutions. In the meantime, based on the special Hungarian developments of the 1970s and 1980s, he has developed a new theory which may be called the Hungarian thesis no. 2. This theory takes into account a new social actor, the class of the *small bourgeoisie*, that emerged as a result of a process that may be characterized as a 'silent revolution'.

Thus, according to the slightly revised Hungarian thesis no. 1 and the more extended no. 2, in Central Europe of the early 1990s we are dealing with two major social actors or classes. We have both burghers and citizens, although not in their classic forms, and we have a real class struggle between them. This class struggle is described by Szelényi and others as the intelligentsia's claim for power and its reluctance to share it with the emerging bourgeoisie. Its roots can be traced in traditional animosity between both classes, as well as the intelligentsia's *étatist* and nationalist ideology, that is, its claim directly to represent the nation or the general will. Although his work shows that the Czechoslovakian or Polish developments have been radically different as far as the relationship between the intelligentsia and power is concerned, in respect of the present situation Rupnik comes to a similar conclusion about class struggle.

> After years of embourgeoisement the current economic and political crisis reveals a society in a state of flux. What sociologists describe as its atomization has also brought about a new individualism. Making money can be despised by intellectuals as an unhealthy obsession with

consumerism, but the new 'burgher' (bourgeois/citizen) will now demand rights. Maybe the intellectual opposition as a community will become less important in an age of rampant individualism, but both the old intellectual and the new bourgeois will help to recreate a civil society of citizens, emancipated from the paternalistic state.[5]

I think that both Szelényi and Rupnik, as leading representatives of the Central European intelligentsia, extrapolate and overgeneralize fragments of real historical and social tendencies in the region. First of all, the 'class' theory of Szelényi has been as unable to tackle the plurality or heterogeneity of the intelligentsia as it has the small bourgeoisie. Rupnik gives a very good comparative analysis of Czechoslovakia, Hungary and Poland, mentioning the plurality of social actors including the intelligentsia and the 'bourgeoisie', though failing to classify or systematically describe them. It is evident, however, that, unless we are satisfied with the commonplace that the intelligentsia in Hungary joined power, in Czechoslovakia opposed power and in Poland was split between opposition and power, a real comparison between those countries needs a differentiation or 'breakdown' of the general and abstract notions of intelligentsia and bourgeoisie.

In some analyses of the 1989 revolutions we see an effort to distinguish systematically between the major types of elites. Karen Dawisha states that

> within Eastern Europe there are roughly three types of elites. Czecho-Slovakia is a country in which all three groups have existed, however without co-existing. The first group consists of those loyal and staunch communists who presumably, would choose to live in a social system if they had to do it all over again. The second group consists of a rather substantial stratum of professionally qualified but ideologically disengaged officials who have sought high party and state positions in order to receive the perks of life at the top of the *nomenklatura* ladder. This group still exists, but their loyalties have shifted away from the communists. The third group is composed of the experts, culturally sophisticated intelligentsia elite. From their ranks rose many of the economic reforms, political demands, and cultural programs designed to serve indigenous national requirements and forge closer links with Western Europe than Moscow previously encouraged.[6]

We see three agents of power and influence in state socialism here:

1 The power elite, the apparatchiks or leading bureaucrats as a 'ruling class' who, some decades ago, may have been recruited from the revolutionary-romantic intelligentsia but who have since then been organized according to the rules of monopolistic power and who have been predominantly inimical to the intelligentsia's demands for reforms, power-sharing and autonomy of different social spheres.

2 The administrative-technocratic, professional elite which has been raised to deal with the problems related to increasing societal complexity. This group accepted the rules of the game (meaning total control by the power elite) but by its influence based on knowledge and expertise it was a threat to that elite from the very start. After the first period of real Stalinism the two elite groups to some extent shared power, the second group constantly eroding the power base of the first. Growing professionalization and de-ideologization in the 1980s coincided with this professional elite manifestly expressing its claim for power. This process took place most markedly in Hungary.

3 The intellectual counter-elite, composed of the publicly known, leading intellectual personas of high social reputation and prestige, visibility and self-esteem, representing the 'intelligentsia' directly. As critical intellectuals (mostly poets, writers and historians) facing the power, they claimed to represent the whole nation with their social influence, cultural capital and political credibility. They mediated between the power elite and the people, at times even successfully bargaining for certain issues.

Out of the situation of conflict between the three groups emerged a counter-elite or alternative elite consisting of leading intellectuals fighting also not only the power elite, but also the pragmatic experts, the professional elite as a subservient and dangerously technocratic class. This counter-elite shows an unclear profile stretching from romantic messianism to realistic social criticism based on the 'soft' social sciences (sociology, political science and human rights).

Consequently, we have at least three major actors at the level of the elites, in some ways overlapping each other. To a certain extent all three fall within the category of intelligentsia. Because the competition for power between them has not been decided, from the very beginning of state socialism until the present time contradictions and tensions have been increasing. Mutual relationships between the groups vary from country to country, the Hungarian thesis mirroring the fact that in Hungary the second elite was relatively powerful, compared with the other countries. Everywhere the third elite became the most powerful after the revolutions of 1989.

The intellectual counter-elite has created its own image of being the 'Hungarian thesis as such' and it has been dominated by the writers and historians, traditionally representing national consciousness and historical responsibility. This part of the intelligentsia has claimed to be devoted politicans and 'servants of the nation', that is, to be surrogate citizens as mentioned before, and act as moral and cultural substitutes for professional politicians. In the growing crisis of state socialism these intellectuals as writers have more and more come to the fore. On one hand, they have become overburdened by societal demands, and on the other hand they have prepared and even signed a social contract with the declining party state and, later on, monopolized power in an emerging elite-democracy. The erosion of state control over civil society and the gradual process of emancipation of society has silently been turned back by this new claim for monopolistic power; once more legitimized by the claim directly to represent the nation or general will. The revival of citizenship and civil society was a precondition for the democratic transition but, changing from an intellectual counter-elite to the organized and legalized opposition and moving from symbolic to real politics, this intelligentsia has fallen into the well-known Central European trap of political representation, using the same legitimation device as its predecessor in state socialism, although using different arguments. Again, a few charismatic leaders decide the national interest. The new leaders, turning moral indignation into professional politics, have very great personal reputation and credibility. However, they have not answered the masses' claim to be involved in politics as yet.

The Hungarian thesis revised

When the elite-literator intelligentsia came to power, it found out that there was at least one more competitor: the (small) 'bourgeoisie'. This social actor appeared in Szelényi's Hungarian thesis no. 2 long before 1989; its entering the scene has been described by different authors as 'second society or second economy', embourgeoisement, pragmatic values, entrepreneurial class, etc. Therefore, we have to analyse the intelligentsia's rise to power from this angle as well, that is, from the side of the emerging 'masses' marching towards (class) power. Although common presentations of the struggle for power between intelligentsia and bourgeoisie in a situation of democratic transition are themselves ideological 'overspill' products of the real tendencies, the problem is here, with us: who gets what from the economic (property) and political (government) power?

A clear answer to these questions has been given by Elemér Hankiss, an internationally known Hungarian sociologist, in his theory on the second society and in his recent theory on the Grand

Coalition, which is a revision of the Hungarian thesis.[7] Both Szelényi and Hankiss consider the second economy, the small bourgeoisie and the whole complex of civil society as very important features of state socialism, particularly in Hungary. Hankiss, however, has always concentrated on the fundamental cleavage in society between, on the one hand, the ruling elite, officialdom and its realm – in other words, the formal society as state and politics – and, on the other hand, the average or common people and their realms – in other words, the informal, second or civil society. For him, it is not the intelligentsia as a 'class' which has taken power, as he sees the Hungarian society as very differentiated. Instead of unified social actors there is a very perplexed and chaotic society 'down' in which the average Hungarian works, to begin with in the state sector according to the rule of the bureaucratic management principle, then in the second economy according to the rules of the market, and finally sometimes in different client and other networks. So, he has to switch discourse, style of speech, mode of behaviour, several times a day and his social status is determined by these multiple, partially contradicting, partially complementary, factors of a decomposing society.[8]

This is not the place to outline the liberalization process or the developments of the second economy in Hungary from the mid-1960s onwards, its positive features and limitations (economic, cultural and social pluralization and decentralization but no political democratization), as they are elaborated in one Hankiss 'social democratization scenario'. Nevertheless, it is instructive to summarize his account of the divergent developments in Central Europe as follows.

In Poland the process of proletarianization went furthest, the economic autonomy of the middle class was mostly destroyed and the role of Church as a social actor was one of the most characteristic features of Polish idiosyncrasy. In Czechoslovakia after 1968 only a small group of the dissident intelligentsia emerged and turned into a 'revolutionary aristocracy in 1989' within the democratic traditions of the interwar period. As a latecomer in the second economy, Czechoslovakia lacks an entrepreneurial class and its skill. In Hungary the efforts towards maximum control over civil society and maximum centralization of state power still left some space for semi-autonomous economic and social activity and innovation. Until the mid-1980s the growing crisis of the first or formal economy was balanced partially by the increasing self-exploitation of the Hungarians in the second or informal economy (resulting in average working hours of 84 a week) in which 70 per cent of the active population participated. Taking *homo economicus* or burgher as the prime mover behind the real changes, for Hankiss this chaotic mass is the chief actor in Hungarian history.

> One of the most important trends in Hungary over the last twenty five or thirty years has been the rise of a *'petty bourgeoisie'*. But this is a bourgeoisie evincing a very low level of individual entrepreneurial activity, although a great zeal. By the early 1970s, two million Hungarian families were involved in this 'second economy' . . . These are skills, which are now very important national assets. We have two million potential entrepreneurs in Hungary.[9]

Hankiss points to a parallel process of a more clearly emerging social actor: the rise of a nineteenth century-like *grand bourgeoisie*. This grand bourgeoisie is a coalition and to some degree an amalgam of three or four important social groups, namely previous party bureaucrats (part of the *nomenklatura*), managers with good domestic and foreign contacts and new big entrepreneurs advocating a new meritocratic ideology. Related to these two processes, Hankiss sees a comparative advantage for Hungary, although he warns of the dangers of the grand bourgeoisie's monopolistic power: 'we have an advangage over our friends of having this large entrepreneurial base, the large *petty bourgeoisie* and this aggressive new composite *grand bourgeoisie*'.

In his understanding, this new 'aggressive' grand bourgeoisie has not yet been connected to the political parties, which means that its aggressiveness has been balanced by that of the newly emerging parties and their dishonest and pitiful party struggles. A 'tribal war' has broken out in Hungary and various cultural and social entities, that started out as competing social entities, now fight each other in the form of political parties. The grand bourgeoisie, according to Hankiss, is an economic and social phenomenon but not yet a political one. He points out that the elite has been divided into an economic-managerial-entrepreneurial elite on one side and a party-political elite on the other. Taken together, the two elites show the contours of an emerging elite-democracy, but the democratic transition has not yet fulfilled the promise to restore the civil society's 'birth-rights' of controlling politics. On the contrary: 'The penultimate problem which we have to face is the vacuum between high-level politics, or party politics, and everyday family life.'[10]

For Szelényi, the chief social actors are 'classes', big units of society appearing directly in politics, whereas for Hankiss only the elites are active in political life. For him there are no major social groupings, and the predominant theoretical as well as practical political question is the 'conversion' of the economy into social factors and these social factors into politics. By this conversion process many contradictions have risen, not only in traditional and previous Central European developments, but also in the recent ones, making the map of Hungarian society even more heterogeneous than it was before. To a great extent Hankiss paints a realistic picture, although there is a double price to pay for it. First, Hankiss' elites are conscious, rational decision-makers acting according to the rules of game theory. Secondly, everything except the elites remains chaotic. Even the 'petty bourgeoisie' is rather unarticulated. Consequently, no real actors beyond the elites are present in this dualistic theory.[11]

In an oversimplified way, but concentrating on the essential features, we have analysed the major problems of burghers and citizens in Central Europe by means of two internationally well-known Hungarian theories. Szelényi and Hankiss show contradicting trends in the explanation of recent developments, both equally realistic in their generalization of actual developments and revealing the weakness of an unstructured, unarticulated society. Even in Western Europe the assessment of social stratification and the explanation of its effects on the organization of the political system has always been a very difficult task for the social sciences. Obviously it has been almost hopelessly complicated in respect of Central Europe's half-modernized and half-Westernized society and politics.

Before we return to traditional commonplaces about the simultaneous existence of burghers and citizens, both playing their roles albeit in disguise and by guest-players, we must observe that both the bourgeoisie and the intelligentsia have been horizontally as well as vertically articulated. Both have three major layers, a small elite at the top, a substantial body at the centre and a marginal one at the bottom. A large middle class is emerging in Hungary as the most important historical process.[12]

The revolutions of the Central European intelligentsia

Revolutions, taken as sudden and violent eruptions of mass dissatisfaction with the status quo, the political regime or the 'order', are supposed to be instances where the 'masses' step on the scene of history. This is a relatively fair description of the Hungarian revolutions in 1848, 1918 or 1956 and of the events in Czechoslovakia (or better Bohemia) and Poland at the time, but certainly not of the revolutions of 1989 in Central Europe. This time the 'masses' were missing and the revolutions were made exclusively by the intelligentsia. I am, of course, aware of the mass-manifestations in Prague in November 1989 (I even witnessed them myself), to begin with the decisive evening of 17 November 1989 and followed by the spirit of Carnival in the streets of Prague which lasted for some months. I also know that Solidarity had a maximum membership of 8–9 million people in Poland and that there were some mass demonstrations in Budapest in 1989 with the participation of several hundred thousand Hungarians (e.g. the funeral of Imre Nagy, the Prime Minister, which took place on 16 June). But old-type revolutions, manifesting themselves in mass demonstrations, street fights and widespread violence only happened in Eastern Europe proper (although without resulting in systemic change as yet). Characteristic not only for Czechoslovakia (where this term was coined by Vaclav Havel), but in many ways also for Poland and Hungary, was the 'velvet revolution'. This extended process of political transition, or negotiated revolution, by way of roundtable negotiations smoothly led from an elite-autocracy to an elite-democracy.[13]

The major contrast between Central and Eastern Europe is that in the latter revolutions are closer to the classic type of nineteenth-century revolution. To explain the relative political passivity of the 'masses' in Central Europe we have to consider that, as a result of the incorporation into the Soviet empire, in Central Europe an (imperfect and fragile) structure of parliamentary democracy was ruined. The authoritarianism of state socialism diverged from the historical traditions and gave neither room for the articulation of political views nor for the organization of political activity. This was a deterioration in respect of the interwar period. Most clearly in Czechoslovakia, but also in Hungary and Poland, there was at this time ample opportunity to articulate dissent by means of political parties. Being deprived of the political dimension in their lives in the following era, trapped into the active and aggressive paternalism of the 'socialist' state, the citizens became deeply frustrated and turned to pseudo-citizens in this new tradition of the atomized and demobilized society.[14]

The depoliticized and demobilized pseudo-citizens in Central Europe from time to time tried to make history, but in their several short-lived revolutions or attempts at national liberation they experienced the very limited possibilities for change within the Soviet empire (1956, 1968, 1981). They learned from the Soviet Union interventions to by-pass politics, as can be shown by the 'silent revolution' in the second economy and civil society in Hungary, the dual society in Poland (Solidarity competing with the government) or the refuge into private life in the deeply frozen political structure of Czechoslovakia after 1968. As a result of the growing economic crisis and the increasing burden of the declining standard of living, people became more agitated but not really politicized. They lost the ability, skill and routine for real political activity, for articulating views and organizing parties.

The literator-elite intelligentsia had presented its claim to be a political counter-elite long before the deepening of the crisis of state socialism. The romantic messianism of this intelligentsia fitted well in the historical mission of the proletariat: both were legitimating devices for the political monopoly of a small group representing the national interest and taking repressive measures against hard-core opposition. The regimes tolerated this counter-elite because of its exclusiveness and prophetism, mirroring theirs in many ways. There is no doubt that the intellectual counter-elite consisted of honest, devoted people and that for this small vanguard there were no possibilities to transcend the limitations imposed on it. Neverthe-less, in its belief that only a selected group of devoted people can lead and teach the 'masses', the mentality of this counter-elite contained the germs of the elite-democracy as it is now being put into practice in most Eastern European countries.

Adequate accounts of the revolutions of the intelligentsia in Central Europe are to be found in the writings of T.G. Ash, notably his *We the People: the Revolution of 89* (1990). An even better inside view may be gained from the volume *Spring in Winter: the 1989 Revolutions*, in which the authors, leading intellectuals them-selves, tell the story of the revolution. The most characteristic self-interview is written by Jan Urban. It is on the Prague revolution, and it is an artistic piece, an enthusiastic summary of events. Urban points out the exceptional role of literators in society and politics: 'The Czechs, and to some extent the Slovaks as well, restored their pride in their national attitude to everything through the Arts. So, coming from this heritage, the Arts in Czechoslovakia always ran somewhat ahead of politics'. This role is a historical recompensation for real politics, real citizens and their parties and their fervour of romantic messianism. But it jumps into the other extreme of being 'ahead' of others, namely of Western Europe, because with this literator-vanguard the moral virtues of the intelligentsia come to power. 'We in Czechoslovakia are about to be, at least in this point, pioneers for the whole of Europe . . . Nowhere else in Eastern Europe has the old regime gone, leaving behind a country in a position and possessed of such a general will to construct a new society. So this is where we are ahead of the whole of Europe'.[15]

A sense of inferiority is often compensated by an unbalanced declaration of superiority. This is also very characteristic of the new breed of politicians in Central Europe. In a more balanced analysis

Rupnik follows the history of the opposition in this region from a general pluralism of the independent intellectual communities to emerging debates and frictions, emphasizing the changing role of the dissidents (from the late 1970s onwards) who directly confronted the ruling elite. He suggests that 'the power of the powerless', a central idea of Vaclav Havel, played a central mobilizing role in these countries, namely it 'provided the intellectual framework for this new approach: from the (pseudo)politics of reform from within the Party-state to the "anti-politics" of the self-emancipation of civil society'.[16] What will materialize from this programme remains to be seen. So far politics has won from anti-politics and the new politics has been very similar to the old type.

Civil society in action

The Central European societies are in flux. The systemic change has started with the change of elites and with a transition of power but it has not been completed yet. A historical opportunity is being provided now for democratic consolidation and real citizen participation. But in this initial phase of democratic transition, we have nothing but a lop-sided and unbalanced elite-democracy. In Central Europe a democratic system is nearly established at the top level: the 'roof' of the building of constitutional structure and macro-politics is nearly finished. Still, there are hardly any connections with the meso-level, (organized interest) and with the ground level (civil society) of the building. Because Hungary has some history of democratization, the ground and meso-level may be more developed there than in Czechoslovakia and Poland. However, this does not mean that Hungary is 'ahead', since all three countries are in equally difficult positions to break away from the transitional situation and start the process of real democratization.

Parliamentary democracy

After the first three elections in the spring of 1990 the organization of the system of parliamentary democracy was nearly completed in Hungary. The elections of May 1990 produced a semi-fragmented party system (six parliamentary parties) and a new government built on the coalition of the three right-wing parties. The new government accelerated change of the elites and completed the power transition. The Constitution of 1989 was developed further and became fundamentally democratic. The newly elected parliament started to work very intensively, passing more than one hundred bills (laws, decisions, amendments) before the end of 1990. The free press openly criticized all actors of political life. This bright picture suggests that by the American, procedural, definition of democracy, the Hungarian polity is a perfect democracy now. However, free elections are no more than a first step towards democratic transition and many further steps have to be made in order to change this elite-democracy into a substantial democracy with extensive citizen participation.[17]

The macropolitical system has formally, but not substantially, acquired democratic features. This is the point where the role of the intelligentsia in Central Europe is at play. The politics of the newly powerful intellectuals is self-centred and arrogant; the political elite only deals with itself, that is, with narrow-minded party politics, and neglects the crisis management of the ailing economy. This results in growing discontent with the new politicians and politics, in other words with the 'trap of politics': politics dealing only with politics. The Hungarian situation is a perfect example. In 1990 the Hungarians had 'free elections' five times in a row, displaying growing abstention. Each time a larger number of citizens voted against politics, more precisely, against the elite-democracy. Six months after the parliamentary elections, at the elections for local government (September–October 1990), the majority of the population withdrew its support from the governing coalition and voted for the opposition parties.

The new democracies in Central Europe have followed a historical trajectory from euphoria to disappointment. A small part of the elite-intelligentsia (mostly literators and historians), organized in different parties (elites and counter-elites), has conquered power. It has brought life into politics its own stratum-specific values and cultural traditions, and imposed them upon political life and on the country as a whole. Accordingly, old debates about cultural traditions, between 'urbanists' and 'national populists', have become the major organizing principle of politics and have pushed aside the much more important questions of economic and social crisis management. The governing coalition has been haunted by nostalgia for nineteenth-century Hungary and the neo-baroque scenery of the interwar period and has tried to restore the state-party tradition (including its conservative-authoritarian political style) from the period before state socialism. Thus, the problems of the new democracy converge in the historical adventure of the traditional literator-intelligentsia and in the stalemate of their ideological fights. The lack of citizen participation provides a missing link in the foundations of democracy and explains the political system's low efficiency.

The functional democracy (organized interest)

Missing in the building of the new Hungarian democracy is a meso-level structure consisting of the institutions of a functional democracy. This is not by coincidence. The literator-intelligentsia, coming to power, favours the mechanisms of 'direct national interests' and has developed a suspicious attitude to any form of representation of particular ('material' or economic) interests of different social strata. In 1984, before the start of the democratic transition, a bicameral parliament, with a lower house for the representation of corporative interests based on a so-called functional democracy, was under discussion. After the transition of power (in August 1990) the national Council for Interest Articulation was formed, which is nothing but a simple forum for public debate. After long political struggle it may eventually become a germ for a triangular structure of conflict management organization between state, employers and employees; the fact that its present mandate is very narrow reflects the government's neglect of organized interest.

In 1989–90 the old party structure in Hungary collapsed and new parties emerged that in 1990-91 became the major, if not the only, actors on the political scene. The old trade union structures have been half-ruined, half-delegitimized, and so far the new ones have been weak and relatively small. Thus, labour conflicts and industrial unrest, soaring in a situation of growing unemployment and a decreasing standard of living, can hardly be managed on the spot, that is, there, where they have emerged. Because of the lack of proper negotiating mechanisms they become necessarily overpoliticized. The government and most parties do not yet feel the need to involve the corporations, as a system of organized interest, in the decision-making processes of the political system.

On the contrary, the government and most parties still do everything they can to prevent the trade unions from becoming real social actors and centres of interest articulation and aggregation. The parties try to win the trade unions for their own purposes and to use their favourite organization for their own political goals instead of allowing them to represent the real interests of employees.

The trade unions are weak, overfragmented and marginalized. Yet they are more important for the citizen's political activity than the political parties. The parties in Hungary may have altogether 200,000 members against 250,000 a year ago. The trade unions, on the other hand, have a membership of over three million and even the smaller 'independent' trade unions have a larger (newly recruited) membership than all the parties taken together. The parties were unable to mobilize their voters for the mid-term elections but the trade unions are still capable of mobilizing their members for industrial action. They do not preach a sophisticated 'transcendent' ideology about the absolute freedom of the individual or about the nation as the ultimate value, but the trade unions talk about their immediate interests. They try to protect their members from the disasters of economic transformation. It is not to praise the trade unions and to criticize the parties to point out that with a party system hovering over socioeconomic reality and without the active participation of citizens, the building of democracy cannot be finished. The intelligentsia, by its values and behaviour, bears responsibility for the distortion of the present elite-democracy.

Direct democracy (civil society)

The particular character of Hungarian developments in the past decades is distinguished by the outstanding role of civil society, or what I call 'the society of self-defence' against the almighty state. The smooth and peaceful transition of Hungary from state socialism to the first regime of democracy was based on the mechanisms and values of civil society and its associations even though, paradoxically, its alliances were wounded and paralysed by the particular character and actors of the democratization process.

The newly organized multi-party system, however, attracted society's most energetic activists, ruined and delegitimized its previous organizations, and stopped its efforts to fight against the new state or macropolitics. In the campaign for local government elections civil society was invaded by the parties, and the interests of the local communities were swept aside on behalf of the 'national' interests allegedly represented by the parties. However, the resistance of the associations of civil society was felt very forcefully at the local elections, and showed in the number of votes for independent candidates.

In general, the new government opened a strategy of popular demobilization, in order to 'tame' the 'losers' of the economic transformation, and weaken the local communities financially to almost total non-functioning in the spirit of the state-regulated economic crisis management.[18] However, the Hungarian civil society's awakening since the autumn of 1990 has not remained unnoticed. The citizens have become more and more dissatisfied with the elite-democracy and with the autocratic philosophy of the new government. They have made efforts, similar to the period before 1989, to change the 'top-down' structure of societal actions into a 'bottom-up' structure. Public opinion polls show that the proportion of the Hungarian population which assumes that it can defend itself against the state has been increasing continuously. In short, the citizens' awakening may be the manifestation of the 'emergence of a democratic Hungary' or the 'invention of the democratic tradition' as it was in Spain a decade ago.[19]

As the major obstacle of democratization, the West sees the growing danger of nationalism in Eastern Europe which, for example, reveals itself dramatically in the civil war in Yugoslavia. The nationalists have been able, indeed, to mobilize the populations to a great extent and, competing with the liberals, they have provided the major ideology after Communism. Two different kinds of nationalism have been emerging, however; that of Central Europe, having a traditional-conservative outlook, and that of Eastern Europe where it is combined with the 'neo-Communist' almighty state. The second, especially in Serbia and Romania, seems to be a long-lasting phenomenon. The first one is less dangerous and aggressive and, although it attracts some parts of the intelligentsia, it can be pushed back in the process of Europeaniza-tion with the help of the majority of the intelligentsia. In general the revolutions of the intelligentsia are coming to an end throughout Central and Eastern Europe. The real turning point, however, is not behind, but in front of us. As the experience of the southern European transitions proves, the entire democratic transition con-sists of two elite changes and power transitions. The second elite change, it is hoped, will replace the representatives of the literator-intelligentsia by professional politicians. The major problem at hand is the consolidation of the newly emerging democracies and the creation of real burghers and citizens, which can be facilitated only by professional politicians and not by the 'enlightened' rep-resentatives of 'general will' or 'national traditions'. The new silent revolution has only just begun.[20]

Notes

1 J. Rupnik, *The Other Europe*, rev. edn (Weidenfeld and Nicolson, London, 1989), p. 12.

2 Ibid.

3 Ibid., p. 20.

4 Ibid., pp. 242–3.

5 Ibid., p. 221.

6 Karen Dawisha, *Eastern Europe, Gorbachev and Reform: the Great Challenge*. (Cambridge University Press, Cambridge, 1990), p. 158.

7 See Elemér Hankiss, *East European Alternatives* (Cambridge University Press, Cambridge, 1990); 'What the Hungarians saw first', in Gwyn Prins (ed.), *Spring in Winter: the 1989 Revolutions* (Manchester University Press, Manchester and New

York, 1990) and 'In search of a paradigm', *Daedalus, special issue: Eastern Europe
. . . Central Europe . . . Europe*, 119, L (winter 1990), pp. 183–219. I focus here on
this recent concept, referring to previous discussions on the second economy and
society in Hungary in a critical approach in C.M. Hann (ed.), *Market Economy and
Civil Society in Hungary* (*The Journal of Communist Studies*, Frank Cass, London,
June 1990), especially the article by C.M. Hann, 'Second economy and civil society'.

8 In his latest (Hungarian) papers, Szelényi returns to his original thesis on the
intelligentsia conquering power and criticizes the Grand Coalition scenario of
Hankiss. I am quite aware that it is an oversimplification to discuss only the work of
Szelényi and Hankiss, thereby neglecting that of others. As they have offered the
most characteristic and internationally best-known theories, within the framework of
this chapter I shall restrict myself to their concepts.

9 Hankiss, 'What the Hungarians saw first', p. 26.

10 Ibid., pp. 26, 30, 35.

11 See Hankiss, 'In search of a paradigm', pp. 187–91 etc. Here he discusses the
very extensive Hungarian literature on the second economy and 'hybrid' society.

12 For 'burghers' even Hankiss contrasts the 20,000 'grand bourgeoisie' with the
two million 'petty bourgeoisie'. We may add that in the late 1980s the membership of
private and group enterprises (i.e. the real small entrepreneurs) passed the figure of
500,000, others having only some additional activities. For the intelligentsia the
proportions are the same. We have about 1.5 million white collar workers, whereas
the intellectual elite is about 20,000–30,000. The relatively well-paid intelligentsia
with some social prestige numbers 300,000–400,000. For the others at the bottom,
who live at a miserable level, 'power' remains a dream. The emerging but very fragile
and heterogeneous middle classes altogether account for some 800,000 to a million
people or one-third of the three million Hungarian families.

13 I have analysed this transition in a number of papers, see e.g. 'Transition to
democracy in Central Europe: a comparative view', in *Studies in Public Policy*, no.
186 (Centre for the Study of Public Policy, Glasgow, 1990).

14 László Bruszt, '"Without us but for us?" Political orientation in Hungary in the
period of late paternalism', in P. Somlai (ed.), *Changing Values in Hungarian Society*
(Research Review, Budapest, no. 2, 1989), describes the stages of paternalism and
presents the sociological data for the depoliticization of the Hungarian population.

15 Jan Urban, 'Czechoslovakia: the power and the politics of humiliation', in
Gwyn Prins (ed.), *Spring in Winter: the 1989 Revolutions* (Manchester University
Press, Manchester and New York, 1990), pp. 105, 134. See also T.G. Ash, *We the
People: the Revolution of 89* (Granta Books in association with Penguin Books,
Cambridge, 1990), p. 156.

16 Rupnik, *The Other Europe*. p. 218.

17 I have tried to describe the external preconditions of the democratic transition
in my paper, 'After the revolution: a return to Europe', in Karl E. Birnbaum, Josef
B. Binter and Stephen K. Badzik (eds), *Towards a Future European Peace Order?*
(Macmillan, London, 1991), pp. 83–97). In this chapter I consciously neglect aspects
of the economic transition since I have dealt with its major problem, privatization,
elsewhere in Europeanization through privatization and pluralization in Hungary ,
Journal of Public Policy, 31, 1, pp. 1–35.

18 We may be a little 'ahead' indeed in realizing the actual situation since the
period of euphoria was much shorter in Hungary than in Czechoslovakia or Poland.
In all three countries there has been a certain naive belief that we could overcome all

the difficulties with a great leap, jumping into fully developed democracy within a very short period.

19 See 'New democracies, the year the votes poured in', *The Economist* 22 December 1990, pp. 43–4, accepting the procedural approach and discovering after the series of elections the 'democracy's triumphs' in1990.

20 See Victor Pérez-Díaz, *The Emergence of Democratic Spain and the 'Invention' of a Democratic Tradition* (Instituto Jean March de Estudios e Investigationes, Madrid, Working Paper, 1 June 1990).

10

THE MAKING OF GLOBAL CITIZENSHIP

Richard Falk

Perspectives

The euphoria of 1989–90, associated with the emancipation of Eastern Europe and the warming of East/West relations, has been superseded now by a very different kind of societal focus and mood, particularly when the global setting of political life is considered. Our sense of reality about the flow of history is extremely provisional these days. Gone are the certitudes of the Cold War, clear lines of conflict, a solidity of encounter that seemed almost certain to persist indefinitely. Gone, even, is the Soviet Union, first, as a presence, and then even as a unified state. With the Cold War over, many contradictory forces are at work, generating turbulence, and one large surprise after another. We properly wonder whether this turbulence is a temporary circumstance that is likely to diminish, even disappear, once a new structure takes hold. Perhaps, the yearning for such stability is what prompted George Bush to speak about 'a new world order', and for the phrase to be so widely commented upon and variously interpreted throughout the world.

If we try to anticipate the shape of things only a year hence, what we now regard as crucial about the world historical situation will likely itself seem dated. Closely related to this speed of change is the extraordinary unevenness of circumstance, perception and awareness that reflects different locations in geographical and societal space. These considerations of the spatial and temporal ordering of experience give specific content to the nature of citizenship as a dimension of political life for the peoples of the world. Europe seems self-absorbed during this period of turbulence, and then adjustment. As an American, I notice a distinctly European tendency in this period virtually to ignore the world beyond Europe. Most Europeans appear to be sustaining a relatively insular posture towards contemporary world history. Such insularity has many favourable aspects, especially if compared with the European colonial period, or with fears about dark forces of Islamic extremism and the impulse towards their control that is currently a dominant part of the political landscape in the United States.

Our ideas of citizenship in the modern world have evolved out of the experiences of the American and French Revolutions. Two elements are crucial: the idea that a citizen has rights that cannot be infringed by arbitrary governmental action; and the role of the citizenry to participate in the governing process by way of elections and through their elected representatives. Without such a mandate from the citizenry in free and open elections, a government lacks legitimacy, and is not entitled to respect. Citizenship is tied to democracy, and global citizenship should in some way be tied to global democracy, at least to a process of democratization that extends some notion of rights, representation and accountability to the operations of international institutions, and gives some opportunity to the peoples whose lives are being regulated, to participate in the selection of leaders. Voting directly for the members of the European Parliament is certainly a step in this direction, but so would strengthening the role of the European Parliament over intergovernmental organs such as the Council of Europe and the Conference on Security and Cooperation in Europe (CSCE).

Because of this historic and normative link between citizenship and democracy, there has been a general conviction that the more democracy is allowed to flourish the better it is for the quality of citizenship. Of course, such a view is misleading historically. The drafters of the US Constitution were as preoccupied with finding ways to contain the will of the majority as they were committed to the repudiation of royalism and despotic rule. The architects of the American polity were fearful of oppressive majorities, an anxiety amply validated in their minds by the French revolutionary experience that showed the extent to which popular passions can produce terrifying excess. The Gulf War of 1991 was one more reminder that a democratic framework may not be able to provide the desirable degree of constraint upon war-making propensities of the state. Such a realization raises troubling questions about how to go about establishing such restraint, if not by way of democracy's procedures of accountability. The elections of Islamic fundamentalists in Algeria generated an anti-democratic backlash by those who had earlier defended constitutionalism and the consent of the governed as a criterion of political legitimacy.

It will make this observation more concrete by relating it more fully to several features of popular support for the Gulf War. In my view, the societal response in the United States to this war assists us in our effort to understand the evolving (and problematic) nature of citizenship and political democracy, as well as their interaction with various aspects of political culture. In the immediate aftermath of the war, almost 90 per cent of the American people gave their enthusiastic support to an unnecessary war fought on a very one-sided basis causing enormous suffering and with tragically disruptive consequences for the peoples of Iraq, as well as inflicting severe damage to the region's environment.[1] The celebration of this war in the United States received an overwhelming democratic blessing (by democratic I mean here a strong base of genuine support) that disclosed a militarist or war ethos rooted in the political culture itself. This enthusiasm persisted for several months, despite many indications that the war did not achieve many of its goals. It was especially evident at the jubilant and large parades welcoming United States troops back to various American cities during May and June of 1991.

Expressing my concern differently, the rights of citizenship, including the accountability of government and leaders, are not enough to avoid adverse human effects if the political culture is violently disposed, and forms attitudes reflecting racial and religious biases. According to opinion polls, the American public was in favour during the course of the war, especially if casualties were heavy on the coalition side, of dropping nuclear weapons on Baghdad. Unlike Vietnam and other situations during the Cold War period when recourse to international violence beyond the authority of law occurred, the violence against Iraq could not be explained as embedded in a wider ideological and geopolitical rivalry, or as resulting from the manipulations of the state, or as contrived by the military/industrial complex, or the media, or a leadership that deceived the people.[2] In my view, the domestic popularity of the Gulf War casts severe doubt upon our confidence in political democracy and popular sovereignty as the normative foundations for citizenship, that is, for a constructive citizenship sensitive to the constraints of law and morality, and even upon an unbridled confidence in a robust civil society as a check on abuse of state power overseas. I would like to believe that I am overstating the implication of the Gulf War for our sense of the interaction between citizenship and democracy in relation to war and peace. I feel that this particular war exposed the raw nerve of the reigning political culture in the United States, but shared to a considerable extent with the United Kingdom. What is revealed is a shallow materialism combined with the uncritical celebration of technology, as well as preoccupations with winning, with violence itself, especially in responding to non-Western challenges, as well as preoccupations that both inspire fear and encourage an endless search for new instruments of domination in the course of the arms race, now, quite incredibly, being continued in the absence of a serious enemy.

Europe seems to be only a half-step behind the United States on these matters. European distance from the more emotive embrace of this militarist dimension of political culture in the North is more illusionary than real. The European political democracies were generally complicit with respect to the Gulf War. Great Britain as noted was an ardent co-belligerent, despite being Europe's oldest constitutional government. Public opinion in Europe, to the extent it shifted in relation to the war, shifted in support of the war as it evolved, and did not react negatively when the character of the latter stages of fighting became known, the stages during which the war came to resemble a massacre, especially the spectacle of retreating Iraqi soldiers being shot and bombed from the air in large numbers during the days before the ceasefire at the end of February 1991. This brutality by military forces representing the UN aroused almost no opposition anywhere in Europe, hardly even generating discussion and criticism. One can only imagine the explosion of outrage if the identity and roles of victim and perpetrator had been reversed! Or if the Soviet Union had crushed the Baltic independence drives by relying on massive military intervention. The Gulf War, as a totality, came close to being an exterminist war in the basic sense that one side possessed a degree of battlefield mastery that enabled it to sit back and decide how much pain to inflict on the other side, all without suffering appreciable losses of its own; the casualty figures in the war were at a ratio that approached 1000 to 1, a proportion resembling the ratio of losses inflicted on the indigenous peoples of 'the new world' by Christopher Columbus and his fellow conquistadors.

Such concerns lead us to become more attuned to the cultural preconditions needed if citizenship is to function in a manner conducive to any kind of minimal normative agenda. In this vein, we need to consider the degree to which the United States as a global actor and as principal generator of popular culture on a global level (McDonalds, Mickey Mouse and Madonna as prime intrusive symbols) is closing off space for other societies to assert their autonomy with respect to the reshaping of political democracy in a global context. Also, what are the effects for Europe of an assertive US geopolitical position, centring around the claim to establish after the Cold War what President Bush boldly called 'a new world order'. To what extent is this new world order a reality rather than a slogan, nothing more than mobilizing rhetoric that seemed useful during the special occasion of the Gulf Crisis? Is this

American cultural ascendancy challenging the independence and autonomy of other civil societies by its global reach? To what degree do rights of citizenship in weaker countries need to be bolstered by some means to question, and even to constrain the use of power elsewhere? The state is less and less autonomous in the world system, being penetrated by a variety of transnational forces (from drugs to ideas) beyond the control of even the strongest governments. Internally, territorial boundaries are now so heavily and multiply penetrated that it is no longer convincing to draw sharp dividing lines between state, region and the world, especially in relation to major global crises that contain risks of war or involve disputes about access to and price of critical resources, especially oil and basic foodstuffs.

At this point, I would like to shift attention away from these relatively pessimistic reflections on the mood that has overtaken an earlier mood of hope that accompanied the non-violent, yet abrupt, ending of the Cold War. Alongside these discouraging developments, there are several far-reaching tendencies that are reshaping the global setting within which citizens act, and exert their influence in a variety of ways, often quite independently of the conflict patterns that shape our grasp of international relations.

Forms and varieties of global citizenship

There are at least four levels to conceive of the extension of citizenship beyond the traditional boundaries of nation and state. First of all, the extension of citizenship to its global domain tends to be aspirational in spirit, drawing upon a long tradition of thought and feeling about the ultimate unity of human experience, giving rise to a politics of desire that posits for the planet as a whole a set of conditions of peace and justice and sustainability. The global citizen, then, adheres to a normative perspective – what needs to happen to create a better world. Secondly, in addition to such an aspirational orientation, and of much more recent origin, is a reinforcing set of trends that comprise the phenomenon of globalization, that is, the tendency towards global integration, especially economically. Financial markets are becoming linked, even consolidated at a rapid rate, capital formation has become more concentrated in response to global forces, and the annual economic summit of the heads of state in the seven leading industrial countries (G7) is rapidly becoming an expression of the originality of the world system during its present stage of evolution. In other words, a series of practical events is happening that is rapidly globalizing our horizons of outlook, including the contours of political life.

There is, further, a third element: the adoption of a politics of impossibility based on what I would call attitudes of necessity. There is an expanding consensus of informed opinion around the world, especially with respect to energy, resources and environment, that unless certain adjustments in consumptive patterns are made on a global level the human species will proceed towards extinction. For the sake of human survival, then, some forms of effective global citizenship are required to redesign political choices on the basis of an ecological sense of natural viabilities, and thereby to transform established forms of political behaviour. This need is not a matter of aspiration and it is not a matter of empirically visible tendency.

And, finally, there is implicit in this ecological imperative a politics of mobilization, expressed by transnational militancy, and centring on the conviction that it is important to make 'the impossible' happen by dedicated action that is motivated by what is desirable, and not discouraged by calculations of what seems likely. Encouraging appropriate activity can alter the horizons of what seems possible to leaders and to the mainstream public. Such a shift helps provide hope, which is needed, especially when the prospects of success seem poor.

From this dynamic of four levels of engagement we can derive a series of overlapping images of what it might mean to be a global citizen at this stage of history. We have, first of all, global citizens as a type of global reformer, the most fundamental image of which is of an individual that intellectually perceives a better way of organizing the political life of the planet and favours a utopian scheme that is presented as a practical mechanism. Typically such a global citizen has been an advocate of world government or of a world state, or a stronger United Nations, accepting as necessary some kind of image of political centralization as indispensable to overcome the chaotic dangers of the degree of political fragmentation and economic disparity that currently exists in the world today.

A typical expression of this essential idea of global citizenship was presented to me not long ago at a public meeting in the form of a postcard to be sent off by as many persons as possible to the United Nations bearing this message:

> I vote for life and non-violence among the world's peoples and for the scrapping of all nuclear weapons. I vote for the right to water – clean water – food, public health care, a place to live, work and education for all the world's peoples.
> I vote for love, freedom and peace.

Next to the text was a drawing of an African woman and her unclad infant child looking up expectantly at her. This spirit of global citizenship is almost completely deterritorialized, and is associated with the human condition. It is not a matter of being a loyal participant who belongs to a particular political community, whether city or state, but feeling, thinking and acting for the sake of the human species, and above all for those most vulnerable and disadvantaged. As such, an African baby is an appropriate and powerful symbol of the vulnerability and solidarity of the species as a whole.

This reformist perspective is a very old tradition of thought that locates its origins in the West, recalling Dante's conception in *De Monarchia* of a unified polity. Such visions usually reflect the cultural and political outlook of the political community in which the person making the proposal happens to live. There is an interesting convergence of imperial visions and global reform proposals, and it is hardly accidental that many reformist schemes on a global scale seem to produce global ascendancy for the state, region or religion of the proponent. Often this kind of vision unconsciously involves a mixture of pragmatism and idealism, implying that a person can promote a better world by enlarging the framework of their own political reality until it encompasses the world. Not surprisingly, then, we find this kind of thinking mainly originating in the United States since the end of the Second World War, a period roughly corresponding with US ascendancy. The collapse of the Soviet international presence has allowed American versions of new world order to gain prominence and influence.

This idea about making the world better through a set of proposals is basically a rationalist strategy, associated especially with the mind of either the worried or idealistic fragment of the elite. It seeks to persuade the rest of the elite that its vision of a preferred world order offers a way of conceiving of foreign policy or international politics that is preferable to the conventional wisdom of the realist worldview. Such a style of idealist advocacy seems particularly influentail after (it tends to surface after) a major war that is perceived to be futile. The most disturbing major war that the world has known in modern times is undoubtedly the First World War, an extended, costly, and disillusioning struggle that appeared even to the winners to achieve very little of enduring value. The Second World War defeated fascism, and was widely appreciated as a necessary, and even a worthwhile, war leading by way of victory to the extension of democratic rule. Hence, after the Second World War, despite the advent of the atom bomb, there was little mainstream willingness to discuss the abolition of war. In contrast, during the years after the First World War there occurred an enormous upsurge of support among elites and in the public for drastic types of global reform. This period represented the high water mark for world federalists and aroused popular enthusiasm for world government. Such influence was substantially displaced by the geopolitics that transpired during the Cold War, a framework for states that saw the best path to peace, not as a process of growing international institutionalization, but rather as a matter of balancing power through deterrence and creating a kind of stability between two great blocs of opposed states arrayed on either side of an ideological divide.

There is a second image of global citizenship that is much more a reflection of these latter trends, especially in the political economy of the world, which is the global citizen as a man or woman of transnational affairs (although the persisting gender dominance in this sphere means that a startling 98 per cent of those engaged in capital/financial operations on a global level are at present men). I was struck recently by this emergent global identity associated with this expanding vista of business operations while sitting on a plane next to a Danish business leader. He was holding forth to me on the great virtues of the European Economic Community for the future of his business ventures in particular. I asked, partly to disrupt his monologue, whether these developments were making him feel less Danish, more European? He looked at me, with an expression of puzzlement, and said, 'Oh no, I'm a global citizen.' It turned out that what he meant was that his friends, his network, his travels were global, that he slept in the same kind of hotels whether he was in Tokyo or London or New York, that he talked English every-where, that there was a global culture of experience, symbols and infrastructure that was supporting his way of life, and that being European, as distinct from being Danish or global, no longer had much specific meaning for him. He probably had to remind himself from time to time that he was today in Copenhagen, rather than Paris or Rome, or New York or Tokyo. His sense of being global went with a loss of any sense of cultural specificity that could be connected with a special attachment with place or community. There is a kind of homogenized elite global culture that is becoming extremely influential as a social force driving the political systems of the world. It is, in my view, the context being set for European integration, and underpins Jacques Delor's conception of the preconditions for successful European participation in the world economy.

In other words, this second understanding of global citizenship focuses upon the impact on identity of globalization of economic forces. Such identity has many secondary implications. Its guiding image is that the world is becoming unified around a common business elite, an elite that shares interests and experiences, comes to have more in common with each other than it does with the more rooted, ethnically distinct members of its own particular civil society: the result seems to be a denationalized global elite that at the same time lacks any global civic sense of responsibility.

The United States version of this outlook is somewhat distinctive as it is often combined with a more missionary sense that the American segment of this new global elite should take charge of the geopolitical management of the world. The editorial pages of the *Wall Street Journal*, for instance, offer a consistent, if unwitting, voice for this kind of perspective, advocating an American-based unipolarity (as a sequel to the bipolarity of the Cold War) to ensure a successful global economy. The *WSJ* interpreted the Gulf War exultantly in this light, arguing that the military victory gave the American leadership renewed confidence to play this global role. Only the United States possesses the will and the capability to reorganize the post-Cold War world and to locate control over geopolitics in the North, safeguarding a global economy that is for the benefit of the North. Europe and Japan need to understand that their role is to provide financial assistance and diplomatic support, a secondary position in some respects similar to that which existed during the bipolar period of the Cold War, but now stressing an increasingly shared responsibility for bearing the costs of US guardianship. It is an interesting feature of the Gulf War that the pledges of financial assistance from the countries of Europe, the Gulf and Japan apparently gave the United States a profit from the direct costs of the Gulf War of anywhere between 7.4 (according to the *Newsweek* figures) and 42 billion dollars. If such a financing scheme for geopolitical affairs were to be made an abiding feature of world order it would help reduce the deficits in world trade. As part of the bargain, the United States would be agreeing to provide security for the system as a whole, a kind of geopolitical protection service, against any emerging challenge.

A third view of global citizenship focuses on the management of the global order, particularly its environmental dimensions but also its economic dimensions. This view is embodied in the report of the Brundtland Commission of a few years ago, *Our Common Future*, stressing the shared destiny on the earth as a whole of the human species. The Report argues that unprecedented forms of cooperation among states and a heightened sense of urgency by states will be required to ensure the sustainability of industrial civilization, a view now extended in the Agenda 21 document developed for the Earth Summit held in Brazil during June 1992. Only by a massive technical managerial effort, coordinated at a global level through the concerted action of states and international institutions, can diplomacy succeed in meeting the overall environmental challenge. This challenge includes problems of the global commons, the process of deforestation, the threats to climate posed by global warming, energy consumption patterns, and environmentally harmful life-styles. A separate influential expression of this Brundtland outlook can be found in the annual reports of Worldwatch Institute (a Washington-based environmental think tank). The introduction to its 1989 volume even anticipated, from an environmental perspective, George Bush's use of the phrase 'the new world order'. Lester Brown, the President of Worldwatch Institute, who oversaw the preparation of the 1991 report on the state of the world, titled his introductory essay 'the new world order'. What Brown meant, quite optimistically I think, is that the ecological agenda was likely to displace the geopolitical agenda as the central preoccupation of post-Cold War politics on a global level, and that this development would alter the way most of us understood international political life.

To some extent, Mikhail Gorbachev had moved in a similar direction during the late 1980s, impressively advocating the importance of disarmament, denuclearization, a stronger United Nations, such undertakings being justified, in part, by their helpful relation to the solution of worsening global environmental problems that could no longer be handled by states, even the powerful ones, acting on their own. What it means to think of global citizenship from this functional perspective is increasingly caught up in the process of making the planet sustainable at current middle-class life-styles, which means making the carrying capacity of the planet fit what happens in different parts of the world, and working to achieve sustainability in a manner that is sufficiently equitable to be accepted by political elites variously situated and implemented by the different regions and public opinions that together constitute the world.

A fourth idea about global citizenship is associated with the rise of regional political consciousness, and it is of great historical relevance at the present time, especially in Europe. It is appropriate to take notice of the fact that Europe, the birthplace of the modern territorial state, is moving rapidly along a path that is producing the first significant political innovation since the emergence of the modern territorial state in the seventeenth century. The Euro-federal process is creating a sufficient structure beyond the state so that it becomes necessary, not merely aspirational, to depict a new kind of political community as emergent, although with features that are still far from distinct, and complete. It is fittingly ironic that the birthplace of the state system, the whole Westphalia line of development of territorial sovereignty and the modern state apparatus and ideology, may also be the locus of its mutation and rebirth, giving rise to a political reality that is intermediate between a territorial state and a globally unified political order. The future of Europe taken as a whole remains uncertain, especially in light of the dissolution of the East/West divide, and the pressure to incorporate in the years ahead the far less prosperous and developed former Communist states of the East. One troublesome possibility is that the consolidation of states at the regional level could create a militarized European superstate.

There is no doubt that the incentives for European integration have been powerfully reinforced by competition with the United States and Japan for control of shares in the world economy. Additional community-building forces have been also at work, and it is these forces, operating closer to the grassroots, that will determine whether this European experiment will develop into something distinctive and benevolent, making this new European reality a positive contribution to the restructuring of the global system. Can Europe, in other words, forge an ideological and normative identity that becomes more than a strategy to gain a bigger piece of the world economic pie? Can Europe become the bearer of values that are directly related to creating a more peaceful and just world? Whether regionalism in this enlarged and constructive sense can fulfil its normative potential at this time depends heavily on Europe, and on whether European elites and public opinion can move from the dependencies of the Cold War towards establishing more autonomy, especially in relation to security issues, and a more generous outreach towards the Third World. The civil strife in Yugoslavia, as well as the difficulties of proceeding directly from the failed paternalism of the Communist regimes in Eastern Europe to the cruel rigours of the unfettered market, cast renewed doubt upon the pace and prospects of subsequent stages of European integration, as well as on the likely meaning of 'Europe'. Additionally, the unifying of Europe would undoubtedly, at least in the short run, produce tension with the United States, especially challenging the more militarist postures associated with recent US foreign policy. This relationship between a more unified Europe, not preoccupied with a threat from the East, and the United States, could evolve in a mutually beneficial direction. One positive possibility would be building links at the societal level, an extension of transnational democratic tendencies in both regions, based on shared popular resistance to both militarism directed at the South and to the effects of the globalization of capital with its increasing impulse, expressed in G7 settings and elsewhere, to manage the life of the planet from above.

The fifth and final form of global citizenship is associated with the emergence of transnational activism that started to become very important for social movements during the 1980s. In the environmental area and with respect to human rights, the women's movement, activism on a transnational basis became prominent for the first time in history. What this meant was that the real arena of politics was no longer understood as acting in opposition within a particular state, nor the relation of society and the state, but it consisted more and more of acting to promote a certain kind of political consciousness transnationally that could radiate influence in a variety of directions, including bouncing back to the point of origin. Amnesty International and Greenpeace are emblematic of this transnational militancy with an identity, itself evolving and being self-transformed, that cannot really be tied very specifically to any one country or even any region, and is certainly not 'political' in a conventional sense, nor is it 'professional', but it draws its strength from both sources. This grassroots phenomenon of organizing for action at societal levels is also occurring in various ways in the South. It is important to appreciate that this transnational, grassroots surge is not, by any means, just a Northern phenomenon. It has as one of its central features a shared conviction that upholding human rights and building political democracy provide the common underpinning, although adapted to diverse circumstances, for the types of transnational developments that are desired.

These networks of transnational activity conceived both as a project and as a preliminary reality are producing a new orientation towards political identity and community, what cumulatively can be described as global civil society. These developments include the rudimentary institutional construction of arenas of action and allegiance – what many persons are really identifying with – as no longer bounded by or centred upon the formal relationship that an individual has to his or her own territorial society as embodied in the form of a state. Traditional citizenship is being challenged and remoulded by the important activism associated with this transnational political and social evolution. This tendency is not linear. Indeed, backlash is inevitable, as older orientations towards political identity are challenged and more territorially defined interests grow threatened. What is evident, for instance in the recent experience of the United States, is an intense encounter between territorial, statist identities and loyalty and more temporal, global patterns of association, often combined with local engagement. That is, traditional

citizenship operates spatially, global citizenship operates tempor-
ally, reaching out to a future to-be-created, and making of such a
person 'a citizen pilgrim', that is, someone on a journey to 'a
country' to be established in the future in accordance with more
idealistic and normatively rich conceptions of political community.

Conclusions

A satisfactory imagery of global citizenship implies at this stage of
social evolution a high degree of unevenness and incoherence,
which is a reflection of these five intersecting perspectives becoming
actual to various degrees through time and space. It is necessarily a
composite construction that appears in many mixtures. Such mixtures will produce many distinct shapes and patterns of global
citizenship depending on the interaction between the personality of
an individual and the specifics of her situation. Further, a recovery
of a dynamic and positive sense of citizenship responsive to the
varieties of human situation and diversity of cultural values,
presupposes a radical reconstruction of the reigning political culture
that informs and underlies political behaviour in the modern,
postmodern West. The extension of citizenship at this time,
especially given the globalization of life and capital, depends on
building and promoting a much stronger transnational agenda and
sense of community, as well as stimulating more widespread
participation at the grassroots, contributing to a process that could
be called globalization from below. It also depends on the emergence of a stronger sense of time, of acting in time in relation to
unborn generations. The overall project of global citizenship, then,
needs to be understood also as a series of projects. These distinct
projects are each responding to the overriding challenge to create a
political community that doesn't yet exist, premised upon global or
species solidarity, co-evolution and co-responsibility, a matter of
perceiving a common destiny, yet simultaneously a celebration of
diverse and plural entry-points expressive of specific history,
tradition, values, dreams.

   Global citizenship in its idealistic and aspirational expression, if
mechanically superimposed on the present reality of geopolitics, is a
purely sentimental, and slightly absurd, notion. In contrast, if global
citizenship is conceived to be a political project, associated with the
possibility of a future political community of global or species scope,
then it assumes, it seems to me, a far more constitutive and
challenging political character. From these perspectives time begins
to displace space as the essence of what the current experience of
global citizenship means; thereby citizenship becomes an essentially

religious and normative undertaking, faith in the unseen, salvation in a world to come, guided by convictions, beliefs, values. So conceived, citizenship brings deep satisfaction to adherents arising from their present engagement in such future possibilities, but without the consoling and demeaning illusion that global citizenship can be practised effectively in the world of today.

The political implications of this line of thinking about global citizenship need to be worked out. In a preliminary way it is possible to suggest a shift in understanding about the essence of politics from an *axis of feasibility* to an *axis of aspiration*, from politics as 'the art of the possible' to politics as 'the art of the impossible'. Global citizenship of a positive variety implies a utopian confidence in the human capacity to exceed realistic horizons, but it is also rooted in the highly pragmatic conviction that what is currently taken to be realistic is not sustainable. To strengthen the foundations for a global civil society to which all women and men belong is to be dedicated to the achievement of a functional utopia, a polity that is meant to achieve both what is necessary and what now seems 'impossible'. The multicultural foundations of the embracing idea of global citizenship provides some safeguard against any reliance on one more totalizing concept deriving from the West, but perhaps this is not enough protection. The very essence of global civil society is the actuality and affirmation of such diversity, which itself then provides the ethos of the forms of global citizenship that are being most fully endorsed. Such a restructuring of our understanding of global citizenship is highly sceptical of the sort of global perspectives of the transnational business elite, that appear, by and large, to give up the particularity of traditional citizenship and yet never acquire a sense of global community and accompanying social responsibility. We must learn to distinguish such a threatening type of globaliza-tion of consciousness from the hopeful types that rest upon a sense of solidarity, a feeling for equity and for nature, a strong impulse to achieve both local rootedness and planetary awareness, and an underlying conviction that the security and sanctity of the human community rests, in the end, on an ethos of non-violence.

Notes

1 The popularity of the war undoubtedly reflected the carefully managed presen-tation of the war, as well as the generally compliant attitude taken by the media, especially by television.

2 The media, as suggested, reinforced the consensus in support of the Gulf War, but the public supported government regulation of the media by a large majority, and would have happily accepted even more stringent controls to suppress news and images that might have weakened pro-war sentiments.

11

TOWARDS A GLOBAL ECOLOGICAL CITIZEN

Bart van Steenbergen

Over the past few years the concept of citizenship (and in its wake 'civil society') has gained momentum in political discussions as well as in social science research. One could even say that this concept has replaced other concepts, like social class, as an analytical instrument to understand the most important problems of our time. Whether we deal with the emerging underclass, the emancipation of women, new forms of social exclusion, the development of a civil society (especially in Central and Eastern Europe), new immigrants, ethnic minorities or growing nationalism, the concept of citizenship is not only used to analyse these issues, but it is also of great appeal as a constructive response to these problems and to the new relations we are facing today.

At first sight, this is somewhat unexpected and for some even disappointing. Aren't we dealing here with something that is 'old hat'? Citizenship was once connected with revolutionary change and in that context was comparable to the concept of 'class' in the Marxian sense. However, that seems to be over if we look at the celebration of two hundred years of the French Revolution in 1989. This was primarily the festival of the '*bourgeois satisfait*', the established order in France, headed by a president who begins to resemble '*le roi soleil*'. In short, it looks as if the struggle for citizenship is *passé* and that we have all become citizens with certain rights and obligations. So one can ask whether the revival of the notion of citizenship is the expression of 'the end of history'[1] of a society which has found its ultimate form.

However, since the 14 July 1989 the history of Europe has changed considerably. The breakdown of Communism in Eastern Europe has raised a renewed interest there in the building of a civil society and a culture of citizens instead of comrades. In Western Europe the notion of *social* citizenship is at stake with the decline of the welfare state and the question of open borders after 1992. The possibility of streams of immigrants has suddenly brought the question of first- and second-class citizens, of inclusion and exclusion, to the fore again. It would be an exaggerated claim to say that citizenship is once more a revolutionary concept, but it has certainly gained a recent appeal and is again something to be concerned about and striven for.

It is tempting to go deeper into the revival of the concept of citizenship, but I shall refrain from that here and limit myself to one particular question which so far has been outside the focus of citizenship but which seems to be crucial to understanding some of the fundamental contradictions of our time. I refer to the so-called environmental or ecological *'problematique'*. Current discussions seem to concern 'two cultures': one dealing with citizenship problems and the other with environmental problems, and so far these two cultures have not met. In this chapter I shall try to bring these two cultures together by raising the issue of the possible meaning (or, better, meanings) of ecological or environmental citizenship.

As a starting point I shall make use of T.H. Marshall's famous essay on 'Citizenship and social class' (1949),[2] which is invariably used as the beginning of recent discussions on citizenship. Marshall's essay is important for us for two reasons: it shows that citizenship is a *dynamic* concept and that the notion of *participation* is crucial. Marshall distinguishes three aspects of citizenship: civil, political and social. This last aspect is especially important, because it gives the formal status of citizenship, as guaranteed by civil and political rights, a material foundation. It was the newly founded welfare state which enabled the citizen to exercise his or her rights to 'full participation in the community'.

Marshall wrote all this in 1949. It was a moment of hope about social citizenship. The British electorate had overthrown the Conservative government and installed the Labour party committed to building a welfare state. Marshall envisaged a state that would not only smooth the roughest edges off the sharp inequalities of class society, but actually *erode* the class-based status differences altogether. Social citizenship was seen by Marshall as the end point of a development that had taken place over three centuries.

It is my intention to explore the possibility that at the edge of the twenty-first century, citizenship will gain a new and fourth dimension. I am referring here to the notion of *ecological* citizenship as an addition, but also as a correction, to the three existing forms of citizenship: civil, political and social.

An intriguing question in this context is why ecological problems have so far been left out of the debate on citizenship. One could argue that it is because we are dealing here with a new problem, but this explanation is unsatisfactory, since citizenship is a dynamic concept and in the past it has integrated new developments and problems, as Marshall's notion of social citizenship has demonstrated. A more plausible explanation is that somewhat contrasting values are involved here.

A citizen and certainly a 'burgher' (an economic citizen), will emphasize his or her freedom and hates to be restricted by boundaries. Moreover, he or she is action-orientated and in many cases he or she sees him- or herself as a do-er, a '*Macher*' as the Germans would say, who will intervene in society as well as in nature. The emerging ecological paradigm, on the other hand, emphasizes that restraints should be put on human actions and interventions. This comes forward very clearly in *Eurotaoismus*, by the German philosopher Peter Sloterdijk, who makes a plea for the opposite of an action-inspired programme.[3] According to Sloterdijk, much would be achieved if we would slow down our urge to act and recognize that often nothing should be done. This is how the title *Eurotaoismus* should be interpreted, a new critical theory, based on a form of Asian renaissance with its more contemplative style of life.[4] Naturally, not all environmentalists would agree with Sloterdijk in this respect, but he seems to point to a discrepancy between the value systems of the classic citizen and of many (post)modern environmentalists.

In *Citizenship and Capitalism*, Bryan Turner has emphasized the crucial role of social movements in the extension of citizenship rights.[5] The movement for the abolition of slavery; the labour movement in the nineteenth century; and the women's, the gay and the civil rights movements in our time have been crucial for the accomplishment of equal rights for blacks, industrial workers, homosexuals and women. In our time it seems that environmentalism or 'greenism' as a social movement will prove to be the strongest force for the development of different forms of 'rights of nature' and also for the development of ecological citizenship.

In this context we can distinguish three different and partly overlapping approaches to ecological citizenship as promoted by different (sub-)movements within the broader context of the global environmental movement.

The first approach emphasizes the notion of increasing inclusion. Here the idea that only existing mature human beings can be citizens is challenged. This is put forward, in particular, in the claims of the so-called animal rights movement.

The second approach focuses on the responsibility of human beings *vis-à-vis* nature. Most national and local green parties and environmental movements express the concern that citizenship should not only mean responsibility for society but also for nature.

The third approach stresses the global dimension of ecological citizenship. In recent years the environmental movement has become more and more a global movement in the sense that the notion of a global *ecological* citizen is developed as an alternative to the standard notion of global citizenship.

Inclusion beyond existing human beings

The history of citizenship can be described as one of increasing inclusion. In ancient Athens, where it all started, only free men were considered citizens; women, slaves and foreigners were excluded from that office. Since that time, and particularly in the past two centuries, there has been a process of increasing inclusion (be it with ups and downs) to the extent that nowadays it seems that in most Western countries all mature and 'sane' inhabitants are considered citizens.

In the context of the type of inclusion we are interested in here, two developments are important. The first one can be found in the Brundtland report *Our Common Future* where the key concept of *sustainability* is formulated in terms of *the rights of as yet unborn human beings*.[6] The rights of these 'not yet born' to a liveable earth was probably the most important motive for the Brundtland Commission's plea for radical environmental measures. Similarly, the call for stewardship by the World Council of Churches is based on the notion of the preservation of God's creation for *future generations*. It should, however, be emphasized that this first type of extension in an ecological direction remains within the framework of an anthropocentric view on the universe.

The second type of extension goes one step further as has already been suggested by Bryan Turner, who phrases the basic issues as follows: 'citizenship is not simply about class and capitalism, but it also involves debates about the social rights of women, children, the elderly and even animals'.[7] It is this last category which is of particular importance, in that here suddenly non-human beings are mentioned.

The historical mission of the environmental movement is not only to protect the environment for the benefit of human species, but also to defend the rights of nature itself. While each of the preceding social movements helped to widen the participation and inclusion of *certain human groups* previously excluded from the political process or from political discourse, the last historical trend, the environmental movement, is expanding the notion of citizenship as such to include parts of nature other than humans. Here, basic issues about the rights of all living beings are raised.

It is, by the way, not so much the environmental movement in its totality, but primarily the animal rights movement which has raised these issues forcefully. This last movement still is, as Walter Anderson has demonstrated, not quite accepted as a serious *political* movement. However, according to him, the time has come to take it seriously, as a principled attempt to redefine some of our most basic concepts about the nature of political rights and obligations.[8]

The history of Western civilization shows a great deal of ambivalence with regard to the position and rights of animals. The Bible gave them into human dominion, the Catholic Church taught that they had no souls. Descartes placed them outside the category of thinking beings, classing them as a variety of machinery; and even Kant, who spoke against regarding human beings as means to an end, saw animals as means, not ends in themselves. Yet, despite these views, which have exiled animals from the network of rights and obligations that form human society, there is a long and bizarre history of animals having been tried and punished for crimes. This can be seen as a remnant of a premodern or even pre-Christian era, but it may also reflect an ambivalence towards animals, a feeling that they are not mind-less and soul-less objects, but somehow a part of the community of moral life.

In the recent discussion we see different motives for the defence of animal rights. The American philosopher Peter Singer, for example, follows Jeremy Bentham, whose utilitarian philosophy holds that justice in society should not be based on something like 'natural law', but on a calculus of pleasure and pain.[9] Bentham is well known for his basic principle of 'the greatest happiness for the greatest number'. Important here is that, according to Bentham, the same calculus should be applied to non-human life, which means that the capacity to suffer should be the basic principle, which should trace what he calls the insuperable line.[10] Peter Singer adds to this, that the only defensible boundary of concern for the interests of others is the capacity to suffer and/or the experience of enjoyment. According to him any other characteristic, like intelligence or rationality, would be as arbitrary as skin colour.[11]

Another leading animal rights philosopher, Tom Regan, agrees that animals should have rights, but he does not agree with Singer that the subject should be approached in utilitarian terms, since utilitarianism reduces the being to a mere receptacle of experiences with no inherent value of its own.[12] Regan defends his position from the point of view of inherent worth and thus inherent moral rights. He argues that 'like us animals have certain basic moral rights, including in particular the fundamental right to be treated with the respect that, as possessors of inherent value, they are due as a matter of strict justice.[13] Whatever the precise motives may be, according to Anderson, there seems to be an emerging public consensus about admitting animals to membership of the *polis*.[14]

So, in short, ecological citizenship in this view has to do with the extension of citizenship rights to non-human beings. Naturally it will remain an intriguing question how far we could and should go in this respect. The boundaries remain blurred, once one has opened the border line between humans and non-human creatures. What about insects? What about plants? However, we should be aware of the danger that such considerations provide an escape for those who would prefer to ignore the whole matter.

The emphasis on responsibility

Considering the role of social movements, there is one important difference between the environmental movement and other emancipation movements. This difference has to do with the notion of *responsibility*. While blacks, workers, women and other minority groups have been able to stand up for their own rights, the rights of nature have to be defended by others, that is, by human beings. This brings us to the point that citizenship not only concerns rights and entitlements, but also duties, obligations and responsibilities. It should be emphasized here again that citizenship is an office, which requires commitment of the citizen for the community.

Up until recently, this notion of responsibility for the community was limited to the realm of human beings, or perhaps we should say to the realm of culture (the manufactured environment), as distinct from and in opposition to the realm of nature. Ecological citizenship means an extension of this responsibility to the natural world. What is challenged here is the primacy of society over nature. Human goals of all kinds are seen as dependent on the integrity of the biosphere. As a result, a politics concerned solely with the position of different social groups or the relationship between human beings, however radical, is seen as implicitly subordinating nature to a secondary position. This requires a different attitude in the sense that nature should now be part of this type of inclusion process.

Here the notion of participation may be helpful to indicate the new attitude of the ecological citizen, since participation is the key concept in the definition of citizenship as given by Marshall. To elucidate this, we can refer to the six basic attitudes towards nature (which can be placed on a continuum) that the environmental philosopher Zweers has distinguished.[15]

At one extreme we find the attitude of human as a despot, the absolute ruler, who has completely subjected nature; whereas at the other end we can place the attitude of *unio mystica*, a sort of unity of human with nature. In between we can distinguish attitudes such as: the enlightened despot, stewardship, partnership and human as participant in nature. This last attitude particularly interests us here.

Participation refers to 'being part of' as well as to being active in and fully responsible for. Zweers has used the metaphor of the theatrical play where participation means that the human being is actively involved by playing a role. He or she does not have to be an outsider, a pure spectator, but he or she should not dominate the play either. Humans can perform meaningful, creative and important roles in the play as subjects with their own identity, gifted with rationality and self-consciousness. In this perspective humans are connected with nature in an encompassing and meaningful way. As distinct from the animal, the human being can choose his or her attitude towards nature; he or she can opt for the role of despot. This participation model, however, implies that being part of nature gives meaning to the idea of the essence of being human.

Towards global ecological citizenship

In recent years the process of globalization has become prominent in many areas and certainly in the two areas which we are considering here: citizenship and ecology. Since the mid-1970s the environmental movement has been mobilized by the slogan 'think globally, act locally', but for a long time the emphasis was more on the second than on the first part of this catchphrase. The actual awareness that the ecological *problematique* is of a truly global nature is very recent and gained momentum after a few threatening events for which 'Chernobyl', 'the ozone layer' and 'the tropical rainforest' have become bywords. The United Nations Conference in Rio de Janeiro can be seen as the culmination point of this new awareness, at least for the time being.

In previous centuries citizenship has been, and to a great extent still is, bound to the nation-state and it is only very recently that forms of supranational citizenship have been discussed. However, the *notion* of a global citizenship is not new. Immanuel Kant developed a number of optimistic ideas in this respect. He foresaw a form of global citizenship based on cosmopolitan institutions and cosmopolitan laws. In that context he made a plea for the desirability of a world government, a loose confederation of states as the end product of historical evolution.

It is only in our century, with the foundation of the League of Nations, and later the United Nations, that we see the very beginning of the realization of Kant's dream of a world government and it is even more recent that the idea of a global citizen has appeared on the agenda. In Europe, discussion of some form of supranational citizenship is primarily taking place in the context of a citizens' Europe, proclaimed as a countervailing power against the Europe of Eurocrats and multinationals. Optimists may claim that this is the first step towards a global citizenship, and they may be right in the long run. For the time being, however, Europe seems to be more inward-looking, which implies that the notion of a citizens' Europe may in fact prove to be a hindrance to global citizenship.

The pure fact that global awareness is growing with regard to both citizenship and ecology does not necessarily imply that we can expect that these two entities will merge in one way or another. As Richard Falk has indicated very clearly (see Chapter 10), we should distinguish between a number of different types of global citizen, some of which are even oppositional to the notion of ecological awareness. This is especially the case with the *global capitalist* as the outcome of a process of globalization of capitalism as analysed by Wallerstein.[16]

There has always been a somewhat tense relationship between citizenship and capitalism. According to T.H. Marshall, twentieth-century citizenship and the class structure of capitalist society have been at war.[17] Turner, however, emphasizes that this is only partly true and only for the notion of *social* citizenship. If we look at the historical process, it is fair to say that capitalism has definitely promoted certain aspects of citizenship since capitalism undermined hierarchical and particularistic institutions and values. Through exchange relationships it promoted the growth of a universalistic culture and by emphasizing the autonomy of the consumer it contributed to the emergence of individualism. In short, 'capitalism thus generates a set of institutions which favour the emergence of citizenship'.[18]

What we see here is that the present global capitalist (global businessperson, manager) regards him- or herself as a global citizen, with a certain global life-style. According to Falk, his or her guiding image is that the world is becoming unified around a common business elite, an elite that shares interests and experiences, and comes to have more in common with each other than it does with the more rooted, ethnically distinct members of its own particular civil society (see Chapter 10). This type of global citizen is the opposite of the ecological citizen in two ways. First, the global business manager's ideology of economic growth is at odds with the ideology of ecological balance of the ecological citizens. Secondly, and probably even more important, this new global businessperson is, so to speak, 'foot-loose'. He or she has lost any specific attachment with place. As part of the jet-set he or she has literally lost contact with the earth since he or she spends much time thousands of feet above the surface of our planet. The result seems to be a de-nationalized global elite that at the same time lacks any global civic sense of responsibility.

The second type of global citizen which Falk distinguishes, the global reformer, might be called a *potential* ecological citizen. Here we deal with a world citizen in the tradition of Immanuel Kant. The idea is that citizenship develops from the city (the *polis*), via the nation-state and possibly the region (e.g. Europe), to the world. In this picture citizenship is an all-inclusive category, in so far as it includes all inhabitants of the world. However, in its perspective inclusion limits itself to human beings.

Whereas the global capitalist is generally a believer in the free market and is not too enthusiastic about the idea of a strong world government, the global reformer is much more sympathetic to that idea or at least a much stronger United Nations. Some form of political centralization is believed to be indispensable to solve the great problems of our time. This vision of the world and of world citizenship gained momentum after the First World War, when the idea of world federalism and a world government became popular primarily to prevent the outbreak of another war. Traditionally, ecological problems were not the first concern of the global reformer, but he or she could become aware of these problems and see their solution as another task for a world government.

I now come to the notion (or, better, notions) of global ecological citizenship, since two forms can be distinguished based on the concepts of *control* and *care*. Control is the key concept of the global citizen as the *environmental manager*, who has a number of things in common with the two types described above, but there are also clear differences. Much more than the global capitalist, the environmental manager is aware of the ecological *problematique* and for him or her sustainability and sustainable growth are central goals. However, what both have in common is a typical managerial and functional approach; the belief that any problem, the environmental ones included, can be solved by innovative technology and creative management. It would be an exaggeration to say that we are dealing here with a 'quick fix attitude', but there is undoubtedly the conviction that this *problematique*, like any other, can be solved within the context of the existing socioeconomic system.

Sometimes a comparison is made with the problem of poverty in the nineteenth and first part of the twentieth centuries. The argument is that, contrary to what Marx and his followers had thought, this problem could be and has been solved within the context of the existing liberal-capitalist system. The recent breakdown of the socialist systems in Eastern Europe are used as another argument to show the 'superiority' of that first system over the socialist alternative. A logical counter-argument is that poverty still exists in more or less pure capitalist countries like the United States, and that it is more or less solved in those (European) social welfare states which are characterized by a high level of state intervention.

For the environmental manager this analogy may imply that he or she has to be sensitive to the views of the global reformer, who is, as we have seen, sympathetic to the idea of some form of world government. The global environmental *problematique* is recognized here as vital for the survival of humankind but, at the same time, this view is based on technical and organizational optimism. The environment becomes 'big science' and the planet is the object of global management which requires large-scale organizations and big government. Sustainable growth is seen here as a goal which can be reached by technical, political and organizational instruments and which does not require a radical change in our industrial civilization. This view of confidence in global management is embodied in the well-known Brundtland report *Our Common Future*.

But the notion of a global environmental manager is only a half-way house in the direction of what could be considered a real global ecological citizen, since what we are missing here is the notion of *care*. This notion comes forward very strongly in the way in which the world is perceived. Ecological citizenship emphasizes the importance of the planet as breeding ground, as habitat and as life-world. In that sense we can call this type of citizen an *earth citizen*, aware of his or her organic process of birth and growth out of the earth as a living organism. The development of citizenship from the city via the nation-state and the region to the globe is here not just a matter of an increase in scale. With the notion of the 'earth citizen' a full circle is made. The citizen is back to his or her roots; the earth as Gaia, as one's habitat.

The former three types of global citizens are characterized by what Sloterdijk has called 'birth forgetfulness', by which he means that the process of one's birth as an organic one has been forgotten.[19] The 'world citizen' as distinct from the 'earth citizen', looks at him- or herself primarily as a self-made person, who is 'master of the universe' and looks at the globe as a place for 'take-off'. He or she has no particular links with the planet as his or her 'breeding ground'. This is particularly true for the global capitalist, who, as we have seen, is foot-loose, and who has no sense of place.

Critics of this notion of 'earth citizen' have interpreted it as a revival of the *'Blut und Boden'* ideology. But this is unjustified. The crucial difference is that *'Blut und Boden'* has always been associated with 'we' (as superior) versus 'they' (as inferior), whereas ecological citizenship is an all-inclusive category based on equal rights for all living creatures.

The exploration of the possible relations between citizenship and ecology has led us to three types of (partly overlapping) options. First we have explored the extension of citizens as subjects. The main question here is whether we can go beyond the realm of human beings. Although there are good arguments for the idea of animals as citizens, it is doubtful whether such an extension would be fruitful, particularly in the interpretation of citizenship as an office, with entitlements and obligations.

More fruitful seems to be an extension of citizenship in the area of responsibilities. This also implies a new relationship with nature on the basis of participation. Such a notion of participation can only become a viable option if it is accompanied by a growing awareness of the earth as our breeding ground. The development of the modern global citizen, however, seems to go in the opposite direction, detached from any specific and intrinsic relationship with the earth. It is for this reason that we have called that new citizen we envisage an *earth citizen.*

Notes

1 F. Fukuyama, 'The end of history', *The National Interest*, 16 (Summer 1989), pp. 3–18.

2 T.H. Marshall, *Class, Citizenship, and Social Development* (Chicago University Press, Chicago, 1977). The original essay 'Citizenship and social class', published in this book, was prepared as a public lecture in 1949.

3 P. Sloterdijk, *Eurotaoismus*: Zur Kritik der politischen Kinetik (Suhrkamp, Frankfurt, 1989).

4 Ibid., 78.

5 B.S. Turner, *Citizenship and Capitalism: the Debate over Reformism* (Allen & Unwin, London, 1986).

6 World Commission on Environment and Development (Brundtland Commission) *Our Common Future* (Oxford University Press, Oxford, 1987).

7 Turner, *Citizenship and Capitalism*, p. 11.

8 W.T. Anderson, *To Govern Evolution. Further Adventures of the Political Animal* (Harcourt Brace Jovanovich, Boston, 1987), p. 207.

9 P. Singer, *Animal Liberation: a New Ethics for our Treatment of Animals* (Avon, New York, 1975).

10 Anderson, *To Govern Evolution*, p. 220.

11 Singer, *Animal Liberation*, pp. 8–9.

12 T. Regan, *The Case for Animal Rights* (University of California Press, Berkeley, 1983), p. 329.

13 Ibid.

14 Anderson, *To Govern Evolution*, p. 224.

15 W. Zweers, 'Radicalism or historical consciousness? On breaks and continuity in the discussion on basic attitudes', in W. Zweers and J. Boorsema (eds), *Ecology, Technology and Culture* (The White House Press, Cambridge, 1994).

16 I. Wallerstein, *The Modern World System I* (Academic Press, New York, 1974).

17 Marshall, *Class, Citizenship, and Social Development*, p. 121.

18 Turner, *Citizenship and Capitalism*, p. 23.

19 Sloterdijk, *Eurotaoismus*.

12

POSTMODERN CULTURE/ MODERN CITIZENS

Bryan S. Turner

There is a common assumption that postmodernism, as a theory and as a social movement, is either implicitly or explicitly conservative in political terms. A rather extreme version of this critique of postmodernism was expressed by Leo Lowenthal in an interview with Emilio Zugaro, where Lowenthal, in showing his disapproval of deconstructionism, the Nietzsche revival and the concept of *posthistoire*, claimed that postmodernism was a contemporary version of fascist irrationality.[1] In more general terms, postmodernism is seen as conservative.[2] This chapter, which is mainly concerned with politics and culture, attempts to challenge the assumption that postmodernism is unambiguously a threat to progressive politics through an examination of the problematic nature of citizenship in modern societies. In making the claim that postmodernism has a progressive, liberating element, I take note of the fact that in Europe (and specifically in Germany) postmodernism is regarded as a political phenomenon which is dangerous in its apparent celebration of the irrational, while in America postmodernism is typically regarded as a cultural movement which is bound up with the liberating element within popular and mass culture. This chapter attempts to overcome this division between political and cultural debate by an examination of the potential for a democratization of culture in modern societies.

There is an important question about the relationship between democratization and culture, namely is it possible to anticipate some democratization of modern culture as a consequence of the expansion of citizenship? If we think of modern citizenship as a type of social status based upon universal norms of social membership, then an egalitarian pattern of cultural participation must be an element of modern citizenship. Although this issue was much debated by social theorists as diverse as Karl Mannheim, Theodor Adorno and Talcott Parsons, in our period this conventional question has acquired a new aspect of a consequence of a (partial) postmodernization of culture. It is not necessary fortunately to explore all of the complexities of the idea of postmodernization.[3] By the postmodernization of culture, I shall mean: an increasing fragmentation and differentiation of culture as a consequence of the pluralization of life-styles and the differentiation of social structure; the employment of irony, allegory, pastiche and montage as argumentative styles and as components of rhetoric; the erosion of traditional 'grand narratives' of legitimation in politics and society; the celebration of the idea of difference and heterogeneity (against sameness and standardization) as minimal normative guidelines in politics and morality; the globalization of postmodern culture with the emergence of global networks of communication through satellites, which are associated with military surveillance; the emergence of a central emphasis on a flexibility and self-consciousness in personality and life-style; a partial erosion of the idea of coherence as a norm of personality; and the decline of 'industrial society' and its replacement by 'post-Fordism' and 'post-industrialism'.

The social and cultural consequences of these changes are clearly very profound. They bring into question the traditional division between high and low culture, because postmodernism mixes and conflates these two aspects of a national culture. This cultural change has had a major impact, for example, on literary studies within the university, where it is often thought that it is now impossible to defend the canon of classical literature. This 'death of literature' means that literary studies are in fact cultural studies.[4] As a result, the traditional authority of intellectuals and universities (as carriers and producers of the national high culture) is challenged.[5] Mass culture which emerged after the Second World War with the general availability of mass communication (especially radio and television), mass transport (primarily the motor car) and mass consumption (via the provision of hire purchase and other forms of credit) has also been eroded by a growing diversification of patterns of consumption, taste and life-style. Of course, many of these developments were anticipated in the nineteenth century by the development of shopping arcades, street lighting, trams and consumerist life-styles; these changes had important implications for personality structures, but in literary terms they meant the end of lyric poetry.[6]

While these claims are contentious, they can be defended by both sociological argument and evidence, but in this particular analysis I shall have to take much of this argumentation for granted. However, there are a number of significant qualifications to this claim which are important to the position taken in this approach to cultural change and citizenship. First, just as sociologists of modernization noted the continuity of traditionalism and underdevelopment in the process of social development, so we may expect traditional and modern culture to continue alongside postmodernism. In sociological terms, there is no need to pose modernity and postmodernity as mutually exclusive developments. These elements or dimensions will persist in an uneven balance. Furthermore, as a response to both postmodernization and globalization, there will be a corresponding (and literally reactionary) fundamentalization of culture and society by social groups who want to oppose postmodern consumerism, irony as a form of critique and relativism in values and moral systems.

The second aspect of my argument is that, while the majority of theorists have taken the somewhat pessimistic position that a democratization of culture is not feasible, and furthermore that the commercialization of culture represents an inauthentication of culture, it is possible to present a more positive interpretation of postmodernization as a process which may offer us both the de-hierarchization of cultural systems (and hence the conditions for a partial democratization of culture), while also permitting the differentiation of culture which is an inevitable outcome of the differentiation of social structure and life-style in postindustrial civilizations. In this respect, postmodern heterogeneity may be compatible with more conventional notions of cultural pluralism. In adopting this argument, I am claiming that some features of postmodernity are merely an extension or continuation of processes which lay at the foundation of modernity itself. Postmodernity is 'after', not 'anti', modernity.[7] In this respect, some features of this account of modernity and postmodernity are compatible with the argument of Anthony Giddens in *The Consequences of Modernity*. Giddens argues that polyarchy, the responsiveness of governments to citizenship demands, will be increasingly satisfied, not at the governmental but at the global level.[8] In this chapter, I want to explore these themes with special reference to cultural postmodernization and political globalization.

Theories of citizenship

Citizenship is an essential component of the Enlightenment and hence a necessary feature of the project of modernity. Citizenship recognized the existence of the secular state and the development of universalistic norms of participation in civil society. Religious bonds and traditional patterns of communal membership were to be replaced by anonymous, secular, egalitarian conditions of social belonging. The creation of a rational social order is an important underpinning of the evolution of citizenship.

Having briefly sketched out a working definition of postmodern culture, it is necessary to indicate equally briefly my conceptualization of the idea of citizenship. In Britain, the current debate about citizenship is associated with the challenge to the Keynesian consensus which was the foundation of the welfare state during the period of postwar social reconstruction by the monetaristic policies of the Thatcher government, and the continuing decline of Britain as a manufacturing economy. In continental Europe, the interest in citizenship is an effect of the collapse of the Communist regimes in 1989–90, the re-unification of Germany and the threat of major ethnic and nationalist crises and conflicts which may result from the de-Sovietization of Europe. The Yugoslavian crisis of 1991 may be an alarming foretaste of inter-ethnic violence across Europe. Behind these political changes, there lies an obviously greater political and cultural issue, namely the nature of the future relationship between Islam and the West. Will the development of a European Islamic movement successfully challenge the secular assumptions of European politics, taking us back into a world divided by faiths? Will Islam be one of the major sources of a fundamentalization of culture in opposition to postmodern consumerism and secular relativism? Will a European notion of citizenship be adequate and sufficiently flexible to meet the challenge of ethnic diversity and cultural pluralism?

While these social changes have clearly put the analysis of citizenship back on the intellectual map, there are two other changes which are fundamental to a discussion of cultural citizenship. The first is the question of the globalization of culture. At its most elementary level, with the growing interconnectedness of the world economy, there has been an associated development of a world market of cultural goods.[9] The communication requirements of both world trade and modern warfare have had the (possibly unintended) consequence of creating the conditions for a global system of symbolic interaction and exchange. We live in a world of nearly instant and constant 'news'. Indeed, we may have moved into the politics of the spectacle as the most significant mode of political debate in a 'semiotic society'.[10] However, it would be wrong to think of globalization as merely an effect of economic change, because globalization also involves the idea of societies conceptualizing themselves as part of a world system of societies, as part of a global order. Globalization implies a capacity for global self-reflection on the part of modern societies. Globalization is more than merely cosmopolitanism.

What are the implications of these changes for citizenship? First, the nation-state is no longer necessarily the most appropriate or viable political context within which citizenship rights are 'housed'. If we think about the meaning and history of citizenship, then there have been, in Europe, a number of important evolutionary steps towards modern citizenship: the public space of the Greek *polis* as an arena of debate for rational citizens; the development of the Universal Church as a religio-political entity within which political membership came to depend on a common faith; the emergence of autonomous European cities in the late medieval period; the development of nationalism and the nation-state as the carrier of rights in the period following the French Revolution; and the creation of the welfare state in the twentieth century as the institutionalization of social rights.[11] At present, there are socio-political and cultural changes which are challenging the idea that the state is the instrument through which citizenship is expressed. For example, in Europe the growth of community-wide institutions such as the European Parliament and the European Court of Justice mean that the sovereignty of the state is restricted. There is a growing cultural awareness of a 'European identity' which challenges nationalistic conceptions of political citizenship. More fundamentally, the processes of globalization undermine, especially in the most privileged social classes in society, the emotive commitment to membership within the nation-state. With globalization, more and more social groups become rootless. At the same time that the state is partly eroded in terms of its political sovereignty and cultural hegemony, localism as a response to such changes squeezes, so to speak, the state from below. The state is caught between these global pressures, which challenge its monopoly over the emotive commitments of its citizens, and local, regional and ethnic challenges to its authority. The question of political sovereignty is of paramount importance for understanding the nature of citizenship and human rights. The traditional language of nation-state citizenship is confronted by the alternative discourse of human rights and humanity as the normatively superior paradigm of political loyalty. The idea of human rights is itself partly a product of this globalization of political issues.

A number of very different but equally potent social changes have made problematic the relationship between the state and the citizen. The feminist movement is obviously important here since, as many critics have noted, the conventional language of citizenship (rights, obligations, social contract and the public) simply did not include women as citizens. In classical society, Aristotle's view of rational discourse and public participation excluded women and slaves as rational participants in the *polis*. This exclusion created major moral and theoretical problems in Greek thought, because homosexuality was the preferred mode of sexuality ior rational, free men in a society where women had a status rather similar to that of slaves. In fact the majority of slaves were females. But how could young men be trained into citizenship, if they grew up in a subservient homosexual relationship?[12]

Contemporary politics have been profoundly changed (although probably not profoundly enough) by the development of feminism and the women's movement, which have questioned many of the conventional assumptions about the divide between the public and the private in classical political thought. Critics of the liberal theory of citizenship have pointed out that, in modern societies, full-time employment in practice is the principal criterion of citizenship, because social entitlements are assumed to rest on an economic contribution to the community. Because the contribution of women to the maintenance of the household is not regarded as work, women are not regarded as real participants in society.

Cultural citizenship

The postmodernization of culture and the globalization of politics are processes which have rendered inadequate much of the traditional literature on citizenship. A central figure in this debate is the English sociologist T.H. Marshall, who defined citizenship in terms of three types of entitlement (legal, political and social) which were institutionalized in the law courts, parliament and welfare state. In Marshall's theory, citizenship mitigates the effects of the capitalist market by providing individuals with minimum guarantees to a civilized life. There is as a result an important link between citizenship, civility and civilization.

It is not necessary to rehearse the many criticisms which have been levelled against Marshall's original theory.[13] Rather the intention here is to extend Marshall's theory by (a) identifying different types of citizenship; and (b) arguing that we should elaborate the Marshallian version of citizenship to include the idea of cultural citizenship. It is possible, by identifying two separate axes of citizenship, to define four subtypes of the general category of citizenship.[14] Where citizenship develops from below (as a consequence of social struggle), then we have an active and radical form, but where citizenship is imposed from above as a 'ruling-class

fundamentally shaped the nature of culture in the modern world. He claimed that cultural democratization had the following socio-cultural consequences: (a) it requires 'pedagogical optimism' in which the educational system assumes that all children have the capacity to achieve the highest levels of cultural excellence; (b) it is sceptical of the monopolistic character of 'expert knowledge'; and (c) cultural democratization brings about what Mannheim called the 'de-distantiation' of culture', that is the erosion of the distinction between high and low culture.[20]

These democratic ideals which assume the ontological plasticity of human beings conflict sharply with the aristocratic ideal of charismatic cultural authority in which the cultured person is transformed by illumination or conversion rather than education. The aristocratic ideal requires distantiation and wants to create an 'elite culture'. It is assumed that aristocratic knowledge, cultural techniques, patterns of speech and leisure activities will be 'unshare-able by the many'.[21] This elite is a genuine leisure class which cultivates 'finickiness and delicacy' to distinguish itself from the mass.

In terms of the historical evolution of the democratic ideal, Mannheim claimed that a strong democratic trend is discernible from 1370 in late medieval art which developed 'intimate realism' where everyday life activities were represented in a naturalistic style. The highly formal and unrealistic style of early medievalism was no longer attractive to new urban groups. Later the Reforma-tion challenged the hierarchical assumptions of Catholicism and produced another stage in the historical development of democratic cultural norms. Baroque culture in the age of absolutism was treated by Mannheim as a reversal of this trend; baroque culture was characterized by ecstasy 'in the form of an intensification of fervour beyond all measure, in a kind of overheated and sublimated eroticism'.[22] By contrast, Mannheim treated photography as the most characteristic expression of modern democratization. Its oper-ating norm is supremely that of de-distantiation. Photography 'marks the greatest closeness to all things without distinction. The snapshot is a form of pictorial representation that is most congenial to the modern mind with its interest in the unretouched and uncensored "moment".'[23]

Cultural capital and cultural democratization

Following Marshall, Parsons and Mannheim, the modernization of cultural citizenship will require a democratization of culture, or in

Mannheim's terms will involve the replacement of an aristocratic ethos by a democratic one. The two main arguments against the possibility of cultural democratization are those criticisms which are drawn from sociological studies which suggest that cultural divisions between classes are illimitable and irreducible, and secondly those traditions of social analysis which suggest that any democratization of culture will in fact produce the inauthentication of culture by a process of trivialization and commercialization. Thus, from a sociological perspective, these claims about democratization of culture do not appear immediately persuasive.

To take two widely contrasted positions, Veblen's notion of a leisure class suggests that the high culture/low culture division is likely to persist in a capitalist society where subordinate groups derive their livelihood through manual labour and are characteristically referred to as a 'working class' or a 'labouring class'. A dominant status group is likely to assume a leisure life-style as a mark of distinction against subordinate labouring classes.

The second example would be that the sociology of education has shown that the competitive educational systems which were created in the postwar period, far from bringing about a major equalization of social outcomes, tended merely to reproduce the existing class structure. Formal equality of opportunity in the educational field was an important feature of the extension of citizenship rights to the whole population. However, the continuity of cultural deprivation and cultural class differences meant that actual social mobility through educational attainment was well below the level which was anticipated by postwar educational reformers. The result has been that the educational system has merely reproduced the culture of the dominant class.[24] The high culture of a society is simply the dominant culture.

Pierre Bourdieu has further elaborated this idea in his study of social distinction, which was a sociological critique of Kant's theory of aesthetics.[25] Whereas Kant argued that the aesthetic judgement is individual, neutral, objective and disinterested, Bourdieu wants to demonstrate empirically that taste is social, structured and committed. Our taste for goods, both symbolic and material, is simultaneously a classification which classifies the classifier; as such, it cannot be neutral and disinterested, because it is a consequence of class position. Personal life-style, cultural taste and consumer preferences are related to particular divisions within the occupational structure of society, especially in terms of formal educational attainment. With the decline of a rigid status order, there is a constant competition between classes and class fractions to secure dominance over the definition of cultural taste.[26] These patterns of cultural distinction are so profound and pervasive that they also dictate how the body should be correctly developed and presented, because the body is also part of the symbolic capital of a class. Because the flow of symbolic goods is so extensive in the modern marketplace, there develops the possibility of endless interpretation and re-interpretation of new cultural products. To provide this service, a class of new cultural intermediaries emerges (especially in the media, advertising and fashion) to inform society on matters of distinction. These intermediaries transmit the distinctive life-style of the intellectuals and the leisure class to a wider social audience. These processes within the world of consumer goods eventually force upper, educated social classes to invest in new knowledge and new cultural goods.

What is the implication of these studies of class and culture for the Mannheimian argument that we have entered a period in which the democratization of culture is inevitable? It implies obviously that any process of cultural equalization or levelling will be met by a counter-process of distantiation and hierarchization. Within a competitive market of symbolic goods, some pattern of social distinction will be imposed upon the market by cultural intermediaries. Although governments may attempt to reform the educational system to provide equality of educational opportunity, there will always be inequality in social outcomes, because different social classes and social groups already possess different types and amounts of cultural capital which they inevitably transfer to their children. Furthermore, because for Bourdieu intellectuals play a very important role in defining standards of appropriate cultural production and consumption, intellectuals as a stratum of cultural intermediaries have a distinctive, if often contradictory, interest in maintaining a hierarchy of taste.

In this sense, Bourdieu's work has very pessimistic implications for cultural citizenship because it would rule out any possibility of the mass of the population participating freely and fully in the 'national' culture. From Bourdieu's perspective, any national culture will always be overlaid and structured by a class system which requires cultural distantiation. Bourdieu's thesis rules out the possibility that a national educational system and a national curriculum could function to reproduce the culture of a society as a whole.

There are at least two criticisms of, or alternatives to, Bourdieu's analysis which we should consider. The first is taken from Zygmunt Bauman's book *Legislators and Interpreters* in which he argues that one important feature of modern society is that the state no longer exercises direct hegemony and regulation over culture. There has been a fissure opened up between the state and the national culture, with the result that the intellectuals no longer have effective authority over cultural capital. They have lost a considerable amount of social and political power as a result. This separation of politics and culture, and the conversion of intellectuals from legislators into interpreters, is associated with the postmodernization of culture, namely its fragmentation and pluralization. The cultural field is more fluid, fragmented and complex than Bourdieu suggests and, as a consequence, it is far more difficult than he imagines for cultural elites to impose their authority over cultural capital. In more specific terms, Bourdieu's analysis may have a special relevance to French circumstances where Paris and Parisian intellectuals have a national cultural function; in Britain, North America and Germany the cultural field is more decentralized and fragmented.

A second modification of Bourdieu's argument is that his view of the working class and working-class culture is extremely passive. The labouring classes are merely the recipients of the cultural products of the market. In his book on *Common Culture*, Paul Willis, following the work of Michel de Certeau, presents us with an alternative view of the working class as active users and creators of popular culture which is resistant to total incorporation.[27] Consumers and users of a 'common culture' constantly change and modify cultural products to their own local needs and requirements. In short, people are not merely passive recipients of cultural products, and 'reception theory' has suggested that consumers have varied, and complex methods of cultural appropriation.[28] Within a more general cultural framework, the arguments in favour of a hegemonic common culture may be as difficult to sustain as arguments in favour of a dominant ideology.[29] This argument is an important corrective to the 'top-down' view of cultural capital which appears to dominate Bourdieu's view of the cultural marketplace in capitalism.

We can now consider the rather different issue of the inauthentication of culture by commodification and the growth of mass cultures in the Western liberal democracies. Mannheim's essays which were published in English in 1956 were in fact originally composed in the early 1930s shortly before the rise of Nazism forced Mannheim to seek asylum in England. Mannheim's optimistic view of the potential for cultural democratization thus contrasts sharply with the view of the 'culture industry' which was advanced by Theodor Adorno, who has provided one of the most sustained and original critiques of consumer culture. We must remember, of course, that Adorno's aesthetic theory was set within the specific context of the employment of film by the national socialists to manipulate public opinion, and that his attack on the culture industry was situated within a wider set of objections to the problems of instrumental rationality and rationalization.

Adorno rejected the false universalism of mass art and entertainment, which he regarded as merely a respite from labour. Mass culture imposes a uniformity of culture on society; cultural production follows the same logic as all forms of capitalist production; real pleasure is converted into an illusory promise. Although Adorno's aim was to break down the division between high and low art in conservative aesthetics, and to provide a critique of the falsification of culture by commodification, Adorno's own position has been criticized as an elitist defence of high art, given for example, Adorno's rejection of jazz music as part of the culture industry. Adorno's form of critical theory has also been attacked as a nostalgic defence of high modernity against the emergence of popular culture.[30] Critical theory's attack on mass culture often in practice appears to be a condemnation of the Americanization of Western popular culture. Other critics have argued that Adorno and critical theory failed to identify the oppositional and critical elements of popular culture – a theme developed in the work of the Birmingham School of Cultural Studies, for whom popular culture is pre-eminently low and oppositional. Another argument against Adorno is that we no longer live in a world of standardized mass fashion. Instead, the world of popular taste is highly fragmented and diverse, catering to specific and distinctive audiences. Adorno's critique of mass culture is both specific to the German context in which fascist groups were able to manipulate the culture industry, and unidimensional in its opposition to popular taste. It is for this reason that Benjamin's more complex view of 'the work of art in the age of mechanical reproduction'[31] has had far more impact over contemporary debate.

Conclusion: citizenship and postmodernism

There is a tension between modern citizenship and postmodern culture. In the context of feudal society, the development of citizenship was a progressive feature of modernization; it was bound up with the emergence of autonomous cities, egalitarian norms of membership and finally with the growth of parliamentary political systems. Citizenship involves the idea of a common status and a national structure of politics. It also involves in cultural terms the notion of a common culture in which citizens might participate equally. To achieve these goals, a common educational system, or at least equal educational opportunity, must be institutionalized. These political structures cannot be easily reconciled with post-modern culture(s).

The postmodernization of culture involves an attack on the traditional hierarchy of high and low culture; postmodernism mixes, conflates and confuses such divisions. The 'death of literature' brings into question the possibility of any agreement about the cultural superiority of various high traditions. As a consequence, it brings into question the traditional role of the intellectual as a guardian of the high culture. If postmodernism has fragmented culture and challenged the authority of elite culture, then it is difficult to understand what form cultural citizenship might assume under such circumstances. To express this idea in Weberian terms, if we live in a world of polytheistic value conflicts, what agreement might there be about a 'national' or common culture which might be transmitted by a modern educational system?

Although there is a tension between modern citizenship and postmodern culture, I do not regard this problem as ultimately without solution. In some respects, the postmodern recognition of incommensurable difference may be merely an extreme version of the conventional problem of liberalism with its celebration of individuality. A postmodern cultural aesthetic might simply involve the recognition and acceptance of extreme cultural fragmentation, the importance of local knowledge and cultures, the promotion of feminist recognition of the significance of emotional commitments to different cultural preferences, and the attempt to recognize rather than to incorporate various ethnic, regional and subnational cultures. Thus, the postmodern critique of grand narratives would prohibit the imposition of national standardization by a high culture and the development of a national curriculum. The de-hierarchization of culture would be compatible with the democratic thrust of modern citizenship norms.

However, the postmodern celebration of difference may in the long term signify the eventual demise of the concept of citizenship as relevant to a period in history in which the nation-state came to dominance. The historical and sociological limitations of the tradition of citizenship may be exposed by the postmodern critique of the limitations of the 'social'. On these grounds, one might expect a convergence between the idea of global human rights, which are not tied to any specific nation-state framework, and postmodern cultural complexity, which recognizes the incommensurability of world-views, the fragmentation of political discourse and the contingency of social science perspectives.

Notes

1 M. Jay (ed.), *An Unmastered Past. The Autobiographical Reflections of Leo Lowenthal* (University of California Press, Berkeley, 1987).

2 C. Norris, 'Lost in the funhouse: Baudrillard and the politics of postmodernism', in R. Boyne and A. Rattansi (eds), *Postmodernism and Society* (Macmillan, London, 1990), pp. 119–53.

3 B.S. Turner (ed.), *Theories of Modernity and Postmodernity* (Sage, London, 1990).

4 A. Easthope, *Literary into Cultural Studies* (Routledge, London, 1991).

5 Z. Bauman, *Legislators and Interpreters* (Polity Press, Cambridge, 1987).

6 W. Benjamin, *Charles Baudelaire: A Lyric Poet in the Era of High Capitalism* (New Left Books, London, 1973).

7 Turner, *Theories of Modernity and Postmodernity*.

8 A. Giddens, The Consequences of Modernity (Polity Press, Cambridge, 1990), p. 167.

9 R. Robertson, 'Mapping the global condition: globalization as the central concept', in M. Featherstone (ed.), *Global Culture* (Sage, London, 1990), pp. 15–30.

10 P. Wexler, 'Citizenship in the semiotic society', in B.S. Turner (ed.), *Theories of Modernity and Postmodernity* (Sage, London, 1990), pp. 164–75.

11 B.S. Turner, *Citizenship and Capitalism: the Debate over Reformism* (Allen & Unwin, London, 1986).

12 M. Foucault, *The Use of Pleasure. The History of Sexuality*, vol. 2 (Penguin, Harmondsworth, 1987).

13 See, for example, J. Barbarlet, *Citizenship* (Open University Press, Milton Keynes, 1988).

14 B.S. Turner, 'Outline of a theory of citizenship', *Sociology*, 24 (1989), pp. 189–217.

15 M. Mann, 'Ruling class strategies and citizenship', *Sociology*, 21 (1987), pp. 339–54.

16 R.J. Holton and B.S. Turner, *Talcott Parsons on Economy and Society* (Routledge, London, 1986); R. Robertson and B.S. Turner (eds), *Talcott Parsons. Theorist of Modernity* (Sage, London, 1991).

17 T. Parsons, *Societies, Evolutionary and Comparative Perspectives* (Prentice-Hall, Englewood Cliffs, NJ, 1966); and *The System of Modern Societies* (Prentice-Hall, Englewood Cliffs, NJ, 1971).

18 K. Mannheim, *Essays on the Sociology of Culture* (Routledge and Kegan Paul, London, 1956), p. 171.

19 Ibid., p. 175.

20 Ibid., p. 208.

21 Ibid., p. 211.

22 Ibid., p. 224.

23 Ibid., p. 226.

24 P. Bourdieu and J.C. Passeron, *Reproduction in Education Society and Culture* (Sage, London, 1990).

25 P. Bourdieu, *Distinction: a Social Critique of the Judgement of Taste* (Routledge and Kegan Paul, London, 1984).

26 M. Featherstone, *Consumer Culture and Postmodernism* (Sage, London, 1991). B.S. Turner, *Status* (Open University Press, Milton Keynes, 1988).

27 P. Willis, *Common Culture, Symbolic Work at Play in the Everyday Cultures of the Young* (Open University Press, Milton Keynes, 1990).

28 D. Morley, *The 'Nationwide' Audience* (BFI, London, 1980).

29 N. Abercrombie, S. Hill and B.S. Turner, *The Dominant Ideology Thesis* (Allen & Unwin, London, 1980).

30 G. Stauth and B.S. Turner, *Nietzsche's Dance. Resentment, Reciprocity and Resistance in Social Life* (Blackwell, Oxford, 1988).

31 Benjamin, *Illuminations*.

Index

Thatcher, M./Thatcher regime, 62, 63, 71
thinking and doing, 67, 71–3
Third World, democracy, 28
Tocqueville, Alexis de, 40, 77, 78, 81–5
totalitarianism, Central Europe, 109
trade unions, Central Europe, 122–3
traditions, national, 33
training, and employment, 70, 74, 75
transnational citizenship *see* global;
    international; supranational; world
Treaty of Rome, 29
Turner, Bryan S., 8–9, 143, 144, 148, 163–8

unborn, rights of, 144
underclass, 4–6, 14–16, 67
    and citizenship, 55–60
    United States, 53–60
undeserving poor, 51
unemployment, 66, 68
    Europe, 61–2
    immigrants, 61–2
    normalization of, 72
    and poverty, 52
    urban poor, United States, 54–5
    see also joblessness
unemployment insurance/benefits, 55–6, 74
United Kingdom
    citizenship, 156
    Gulf War (1991), 129–30
    poverty, 60
    racism, 62
    Thatcherism, 62, 63, 71
United Nations, 132, 148, 149
    Conference on the Environment (Rio 1992), 8, 135, 147
United States
    civil citizenship, 55, 90–107
    cultural imperialism, 130–1, 165
    and Europe, 137
    geopolitical control, 135
    and global economy, 135, 137
    Gulf War (1991), 128–30
    multicultural society, 27, 29, 60
    social citizenship, 49–65
    subordination of women, 81–5
    underclass, 4–5
universal welfare, 93
The Unknown Society (TUS), 44

Urban, Jan, 119
USSR, 127
    and Central Europe, 118
utilitarianism, and animal rights, 145–6
utopian globalism, 140

values, and underclass, 16
van Gunsteren, Herman, 1, 2, 36–48
van Steenbergen, Bart, 1–9, 141–52
Veblen, Thorstein, 162
velvet revolution, 118
violence
    Gulf War (1991), 128–30
    non-violence, 140
    see also militarism; war
virtue in republic, 42, 45
vocational training, 74
Vogel, Ursula, 5–6, 76–89
voluntariness, 25
voluntary work, 72

wage costs, 68
wages
    equal pay, 73
    and family, 73, 99
    minimum, 73
Wall Street Journal, 135
Wallerstein, I., 148
war, 133–4
    Cold War, 127
    Gulf War (1991), 128–30
    and world government, 149
    see also militarism; violence
welfare
    as charity, 101–5
    and civil rights, 102–3
    as contract, 101–5
    as property rights, 103–4
    and social rights, 90–1
    universal, 93
    and work, 66–75
welfare culture/ethos, 53
welfare programmes
    Europe, 63
    effect of, 52–3
    United States, 50–3, 54
welfare rights, 12, 13, 37
welfare state, 2–3, 5, 38, 62, 67–8
    and social citizenship, 75, 90
    United States, 94